Ulster and the First World War

NORTHERN IRELAND WAR MEMORIAL

Published in 2014 by
Northern Ireland War Memorial, 21 Talbot Street Belfast BT1 2LD
www.niwarmemorial.org

ISBN 978-0-9929301-3-4

Design by John McMillan
Printed by Nicholson & Bass Ltd

Ulster and the First World War

Jonathan Bardon

Acknowledgements

The author and the Council of the Northern Ireland War Memorial (NIWM) would like to thank Richard Doherty, Ciaran Elizabeth Doran, Simon Doran, Ben Fagan, Victoria Gibson, Jenny Haslett, Bruce Marshall, Kerry McIvor, John McMillan, Pat McMillan, Philip Orr, Trevor Parkhill, William Porter and Bryan Rutledge for their help with this publication.

Special thanks are paid to NIWM volunteers Lisa Lavery and Anna Marshall who undertook research for this publication, acquiring images from local museums and archives to complement the text and associated lectures.

Thanks also to Ian Montgomery at the Public Record Office of Northern Ireland (PRONI) who granted privileged access to the vast First World War sources at PRONI, which feature significantly in this publication.

For their assistance with images NIWM would like to thank: Gavin Glass, Curator of the Royal Ulster Rifles Museum, Carol Walker and Claire McWhirter at the Somme Heritage Centre, Elaine Flanigan, Keeper of Collections at the Irish Linen Centre & Lisburn Museum, Anthony Richards, Head of Documents and Sound at the Imperial War Museum and Tony Boyle, Collections Assistant at Derry City Council Heritage and Museum Service.

Picture Credits

Every attempt has been made to contact picture credit holders. Credits are noted by the relevant picture. If there is no picture credit the picture belongs to the NIWM collection or is in the public domain.

Front cover/Inside covers
Cover/Inside covers images reproduced with kind permission of
■ Titterington family and ■ Public Record Office of Northern Ireland (PRONI D2966/121/12, T3494 and D3431)

Back cover:
Objects and photographs from ■ Royal Ulster Rifles Museum and ■ Northern Ireland War Memorial collection

The author and the Council of NIWM would like to thank the following for permission to use images:

■ Derry City Council Heritage Museum Service ■ Somme Heritage Centre
■ Irish Linen Centre & Lisburn Museum ■ The Imperial War Museum
■ Getty Images ■ Deputy Keeper of the Records, PRONI
■ Royal Ulster Rifles Museum ■ National Museums Northern Ireland
■ The Doran, McGuckian, Porter, and Titterington families

Foreword

The Northern Ireland War Memorial, according to its founding principles in 1947, exists 'to honour the memory of the people of Northern Ireland who had been killed in the First and Second World Wars.'

At once this raises two interesting points: firstly, Northern Ireland as a separate political unit did not exist in 1914–18; and secondly, the term 'First World War' was only coming into common usage in 1947. (President Roosevelt seems to have been the first statesman to adopt it, in 1941.)

As this book's title makes clear, it is the province of Ulster which is dealt with, but the author is always mindful of the Irish context, and the effect of the conflict on Irish politics. In fact, the post-war partition of Ireland had much in common with the results of the war on many other countries, as the former European power-blocks fractured and new states were created.

Jonathan Bardon successfully combines a longer view of the war with more specific personal particulars of service and, much too often, loss. There are also interesting reflections on the effect of the war on industry and farming in Ulster.

He is a sure-footed guide to times which still resonate today, both in the political arena, with 'the decade of centenaries', and in the depths of family memories. The War Memorial is finding that there never has been as great a public interest in the era, and this publication is a splendid addition to our resources.

Ian Wilson
Chairman, Northern Ireland War Memorial

CONTENTS

Chapter 1 A PROVINCE ON THE BRINK OF CIVIL WAR

Home Rule promised: 'I personally thank God that I have lived to see this day'

At the beginning of the year 1914 civil war in Ireland – not a general European war – was what the Westminster government most feared. Herbert H Asquith, Prime Minister of the United Kingdom of Great Britain and Ireland, had introduced the Third Irish Home Rule Bill two years before. This was designed to grant Ireland a form of devolution (setting up a Dublin parliament with control over local affairs, similar to that possessed by the Scottish parliament in Edinburgh a hundred years later). This plunged the United Kingdom into the most acute political crisis it had experienced for generations.

Herbert Henry Asquith
Prime Minister

Why? The Protestants of Ulster, with very few exceptions, were implacably opposed to Home Rule. Amongst other things, these unionists feared that a Dublin parliament would tax the prosperous northern province to subsidise impoverished farmers in the south and west of Ireland; and they were convinced that, for Irish nationalists, this was only the first step towards outright independence. Above all, they believed that Home Rule would result in 'Rome Rule', that a parliament in Dublin dominated by Catholics would undermine Protestant 'liberties'.

John Redmond, Leader of the Irish Parliamentary Party, (1917).

Caricature of John Redmond in *Vanity Fair* 7th July 1904.

PRONI INF/7/A/2/53

Sketch of scene in House of Commons during a Home Rule debate.

For John Redmond, leader of the Irish Parliamentary Party at Westminster, Home Rule promised to be the dawn of a new age, the fulfilment of a dream long held by the majority of Irish people. At first Home Rule seemed certain. Asquith's Liberal government needed the support of these Irish Nationalist MPs to be sure of a majority in the Commons: to stay in power, the Liberals had no choice but to put forward a Home Rule Bill. In the past the House of Lords had been able to stop Home Rule – even when the House of Commons had voted in favour of it in 1893 – but since the 1911 Parliament Act the peers of the realm could only delay and not reject outright a Bill passed by MPs in the lower house. On 11th April 1912 the Home Rule Bill had been introduced by Asquith who explained that it would maintain 'unimpaired, and beyond reach of challenge or question, the supremacy, absolute and sovereign, of the imperial parliament'. 'If I may say so reverently', Redmond said to the House of Commons with evident emotion, 'I personally thank God that I have lived to see this day'[1]. As expected, the Lords threw out this Home Rule Bill, though it had passed by a comfortable majority in the Commons. The Lords could only delay the passing of the Bill for a maximum of three successive sessions (roughly two years). The Irish seemed certain to get Home Rule by the autumn of 1914. However, opponents of Home Rule made very good use of the two years grace given to them by the peers of the realm.

Ulster Unionists planned to do all that they could to stop Home Rule. Their campaign was led by Sir Edward Carson, a celebrated lawyer from Dublin who had been a minister of a previous Conservative government. Carson's tall frame commanded

[1] A T Q Stewart, *The Ulster Crisis*, London, 1967, p.58; Robert Kee, *The Green Flag*, London, 1989, vol 2, p. 175

Sir Edward Carson

Captain James Craig

respect and the grim set of his lower jaw seemed to show northern loyalists that he would not yield in championing their cause. 'James Craig did all the work and I got all the credit', Carson later observed with much truth. The seventh child of a self-made whiskey distiller, Captain James Craig, Unionist MP for East Down, masterminded resistance to Home Rule and was Carson's partner rather than his second-in-command.

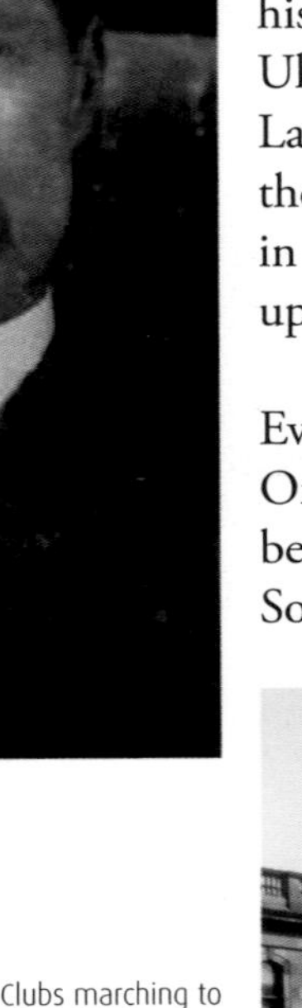

Andrew Bonar Law, leader of the Conservative Party.

Though they represented no more than a quarter of the people of Ireland, Ulster Unionists had a powerful ally – the Conservative opposition at Westminster. Andrew Bonar Law, the Conservative leader, was of Ulster Protestant stock though he had spent most of his life in New Brunswick, Canada, and Scotland. He travelled to Ulster almost every weekend to visit his father in Coleraine. Bonar Law and the Conservatives were certain that giving a parliament to the Irish would set a precedent for granting parliaments to others – in India, especially – and begin the disintegration of the empire upon which the sun then never set.

Events moved towards potential conflict with alarming speed. On Easter Tuesday 1912 over 100,000 loyalists met and marched before 70 Conservative and Unionist MPs in the Agricultural Society's showgrounds at Balmoral in south Belfast. There, after the

PRONI – NF/7/A/2/8

Unionist Clubs marching to Balmoral demonstration past Belfast City Hall 9th April 1912.

THE ANTI-HOME RULE DEMONSTRATION AT BELFAST

THE MARCH — THE MEETING — THE MOTION

A tremendous demonstration by Ulster loyalists was held in Belfast on Tuesday, an army of 86,000 drilled men marching past Mr. Bonar Law, while the total number of persons participating in the demonstration is estimated at 200,000. The most impressive moment of the day occurred at the meeting that followed, when, after Mr. Law's speech and the Primate's prayer, the crowd—in response to Sir Edward Carson's invitation—raised their hands and took the oath—"Never, under any circumstances, will we submit to Home Rule!"

Press cuttings from *The Graphic* 13th April 1912 relating to Balmoral demonstration 1912.

largest Union flag ever woven had been unfolded, Bonar Law told them: 'Once again you hold the pass, the pass for the Empire… The Government have erected by their Parliament Act a boom against you to shut you off from the help of the British people. You will burst that boom'.[2]

At Belfast City Hall 2,500 members of Unionist Clubs of Ireland guarded the grounds. They were organised in sections of 500, all under the command of Major (later Colonel) Fred H Crawford, organiser of the 1914 gun-running. The photograph shows a section of these guards, with staves, taking up position. The inscription on the red, white and blue armbands is 'City Hall guard'.

PRONI - INF/7/A/2/32

PRONI - INF/7/A/2/11

Carson and Bonar Law at Balmoral Demonstration 9th April 1912.

Ulster Day: finding 'all means which may be found necessary to defeat the present conspiracy'

PRONI- INF/7/A/2/44

Belfast City Hall and grounds on 'Ulster Day'.

Then, on Saturday 28th September 1912, 'Ulster Day', came the climax of the campaign. Altogether just under half a million men and women signed the Ulster Solemn League and Covenant, or the equivalent women's declaration. The signatories pledged themselves to use 'all means which may be found necessary to defeat the present conspiracy to set up a Home Rule Parliament in Ireland'.

[2] Geoffrey Buckland, *James Craig, Lord Craigavon*, Dublin, 1980, p. 14; A T Q Stewart, 1967, p.49

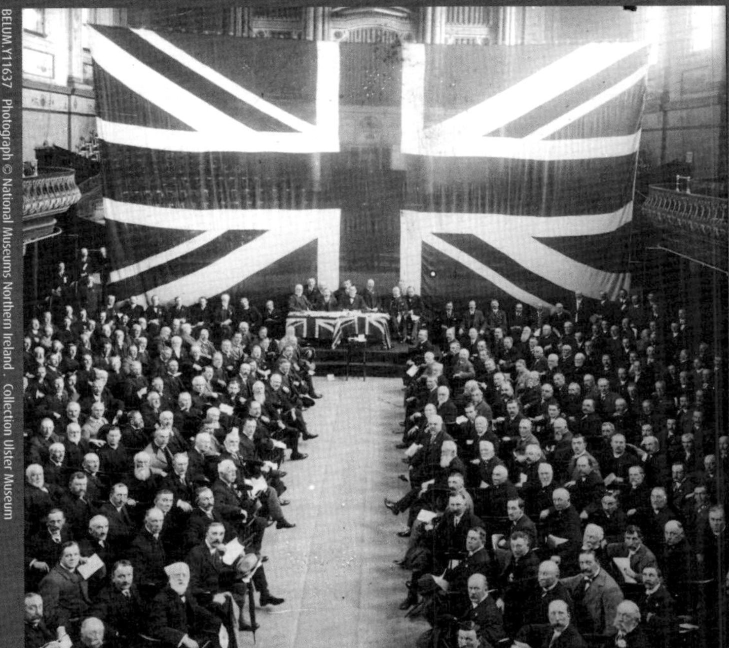

The meeting in the Ulster Hall to endorse the text of the Ulster Covenant, September 1912. The platform party in the Ulster Hall are backed by the 'largest Union Jack ever made' which may or may not be the same one which flew over the Balmoral review in April. The Ulster Hall flag was apparently 48 feet by 25 feet (14.6 × 7.6m) in size. This meeting of the Ulster Unionist Council endorsed the text and a box can be seen in front of the platform party, which was used for members to record their vote.

Sir Edward Carson signing the Covenant, City Hall, Belfast, 28th September 1912. Also pictured are Lord Charles Beresford and Lord Londonderry, and to the right Captain Craig (Lord Craigavon), Mr J. H. Campbell, K.C., (Lord Glenavy) and Dr William Gibson.

Ulster's

Solemn League and Covenant.

Being convinced in our consciences that Home Rule would be disastrous to the material well-being of Ulster as well as of the whole of Ireland, subversive of our civil and religious freedom, destructive of our citizenship and perilous to the unity of the Empire, we, whose names are underwritten, men of Ulster, loyal subjects of His Gracious Majesty King George V., humbly relying on the God whom our fathers in days of stress and trial confidently trusted, do hereby pledge ourselves in solemn Covenant throughout this our time of threatened calamity to stand by one another in defending for ourselves and our children our cherished position of equal citizenship in the United Kingdom and in using all means which may be found necessary to defeat the present conspiracy to set up a Home Rule Parliament in Ireland. ¶ And in the event of such a Parliament being forced upon us we further solemnly and mutually pledge ourselves to refuse to recognise its authority. ¶ In sure confidence that God will defend the right we hereto subscribe our names. ¶ And further, we individually declare that we have not already signed this Covenant.

The above was signed by me at ____________
"Ulster Day," Saturday, 28th September, 1912.

Edward Carson

God Save the King.

Carson's souvenir parchment

What exactly was meant by 'all means'? The Ulster Unionist Council published its plans to set up a 'provisional government' of Ulster. Already loyalists had been drilling and in January 1913 the Ulster Volunteer Force was formally instituted. Recruited from men who had signed the Covenant, it had 90,000 in its ranks by the end of the year.

IWM – Q81759

Sir Edward Carson and F E Smith inspecting members of the UVF (founded in 1913 by the Ulster Unionist Council to resist the implementation of Home Rule)

William Ewart Gladstone

The ground was being cut inexorably from beneath the Nationalists' feet. Unlike the former Liberal Prime Minister, William Ewart Gladstone, who had put forward the first two Home Rule Bills, Asquith did not have a passionate belief in the virtues of devolution for Ireland. He and most of his colleagues were attempting to steer the Third Home Rule Bill through Westminster primarily to stay in office by keeping Redmond on board, and then to get on with other urgent matters. 'I have never heard that orange bitters will mix with Irish whiskey', a Liberal backbencher had declared in an unsuccessful attempt in 1912 to exclude the four most Protestant

Getty Images - 79665274

Winston Churchill as First Lord of Admiralty in 1914.

David Lloyd George

counties of Ulster from Home Rule.[3] Actually, right from the start, two government ministers, Winston Churchill and David Lloyd George, privately thought partition was a good idea.

In 1913 Asquith put forward proposals for the 'temporary exclusion' of some Ulster counties from the jurisdiction of a Dublin parliament. This was to the liking neither of Redmond or Carson. Asquith's indecisiveness undoubtedly helped to make the crisis worse – he more than once described his policy towards Ireland as 'wait-and-see' and at other times as 'masterly inactivity'. In any case, the 'Ulster Crisis' was fatally distracting the Westminster government from dangerously dark clouds gathering further afield.

At that very moment on the other side of Europe the world was being given a grim demonstration of what could happen in an all-out conflict in a deeply-divided society. Balkan wars, characterised by merciless ethnic slaughter on a biblical scale, had been raging since the autumn of 1912. By June 1913 no fewer than 200,000 combatants had fallen in addition to tens of thousands of unarmed men, women and children savagely cut down, mutilated or raped, simply for being – as they would say in Ulster – 'the other sort'.

---

[3] A T Q Stewart, 1967, p. 59

[4] Misha Glenny, *The Balkans 1804–1999*, London, 1999, pp 228–248

Since the only great power involved was the sprawling but sickly Ottoman Empire, statesmen in St Petersburg, Vienna, Berlin, Paris, Rome and London were not overly-concerned by these Balkan convulsions. Again and again for very nearly a century, ever since the Battle of Waterloo in 1815, diplomats had been able to avoid an all-out European war.

In *The Times* and other London newspapers, Ireland occupied many more column inches than perplexing blood-letting in south-eastern Europe.

Gun-running and toiling 'round the muddy byways of Fermanagh and Tyrone'

Book of sketches of UVF Gunrunning.

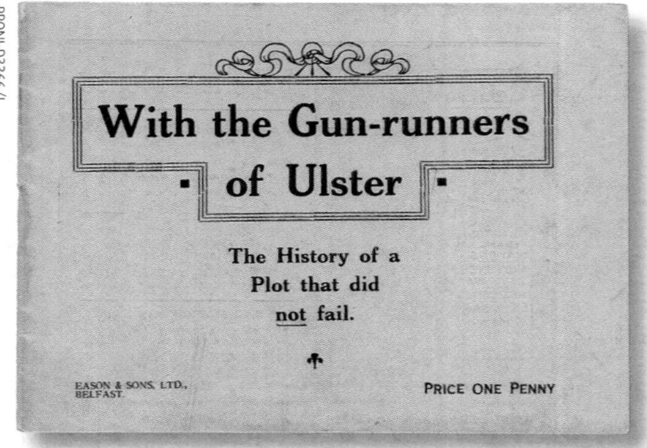

PRONI-D3366/1

Ireland lurched closer to civil war when nationalists, as a response to rapid growth of the Ulster Volunteer Force, set up the Irish Volunteers in Dublin in November 1913. This was largely the initiative of Eoin MacNeill, a Glens of Antrim academic educated at St Malachy's College in Belfast. Amongst the earliest and most enthusiastic recruits to the Irish Volunteers were Ulstermen. Belfast Irish Volunteers marched up and down the Lower Falls Road in Belfast, separated in places by only a few hundred yards from UVF units drilling up and down the Shankill Road.

Ulster had a regular garrison of at least brigade strength. Were there enough troops stationed in the province to be certain that the Westminster government could enforce its will there? Faced with the threat of an illegal provisional government in Belfast backed by armed men, Asquith decided in March 1914 to move additional regular troops into Ulster. Foot soldiers arrived by boat and train in Dundalk and Belfast without any opposition but cavalry officers, based in the Curragh Camp in Kildare, declared that they would 'resign their commissions' rather than take action against the Ulster Volunteers. Though described then as an 'incident', it was actually very close to being mutiny. Failure to take appropriate action against the cavalry officers led to the dismissal of the War Minister, J E B Seely, but by then it was too late. The impotence of the government had been revealed.

D1540/3/94.

O. Form. C. I. A.

ULSTER VOLUNTEER FORCE.

(For the Preservation of the Peace).

County or City Down District S. Down Locality Warrenpoint

Organization Number*

Surname Nugent Christian Name Arthur

Age 17

Profession, Trade, or Occupation Carpenter

Address Donaghaguy House . Warrenpoint

Married or Single Single

I, the undersigned, hereby declare that I agree to serve in the above Force, and to obey the orders of my Superior Officers, throughout the crisis created by the passage into Law of the Home Rule Bill at present before Parliament, or in any previous emergency, for the mutual protection of all Loyalists, and generally to keep the Peace. This agreement shall hold good until I notify my resignation to my Superior Officer in writing.

GOD SAVE THE KING.

Too young to sign Covenant on proper day – R.H.

Signed Arthur Nugent

Witness John T. Bond

Date 26th August 1914

Approved Roger Hall

*To be filled in at County Headquarters.

PRONI- D1540/3/94

UVF membership form signed by Arthur Nugent aged 17, with a note explaining he was too young to sign the covenant.

Eoin MacNeill, commander-in-chief of the Irish Volunteers

PRONI- INF/7/A/3/24

UVF drilling in North Belfast, c.1913

Unknown to the government, the Ulster Unionist Council had formed a secret committee as far back as November 1910 to oversee the buying of weapons from arms dealers and the formation of an Ulster army. The Council's principal agent was Major Fred Crawford who, using an alias, on 22nd November 1910 had written to five arms manufacturers (including Steyr, and Deutsche Waffen und Munitionsfabriken) seeking a quotation for 20,000 rifles and a million rounds of ammunition.[5] Finally, after many setbacks and adventures, Crawford bought 216 tons of arms from the Hamburg dealer, Benny Spiro. On 30th March 1914 Crawford sailed into the Baltic Sea, through the Kattegat and into the North Sea. Learning that Crawford's ship (the SS *Fanny*) had been recognised, the Ulster Unionist Council bought another one for him, the *Clydevalley*. The arms were transferred in the dark off the coast of Wexford while men of the Ulster Volunteer Force were called out on a test mobilisation.

Gun running map – UVF Post Services 3rd January 1914

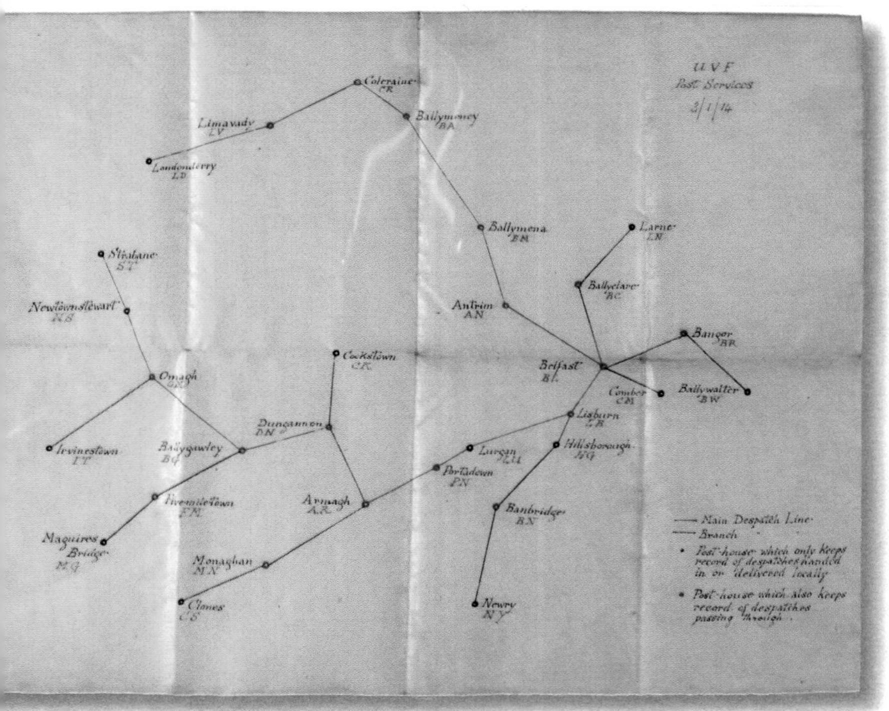

Jonathan Bardon Private Collection

On the night of 24/25th April 1914 the guns were landed at Larne, Bangor and Donaghadee. Altogether 24,600 modern rifles and five million rounds of ammunition were loaded on to motorcars which sped through the small hours distributing them to prepared dumps all over the province. Probably for the first time in history motor vehicles had been used on a large scale for a military purpose, and with striking success. The Royal Navy had been caught unawares. This successful gunrunning caused Asquith's government acute embarrassment. Even Redmond thought that it would now be a mistake to try to take weapons away from the UVF. [6]

It was no surprise that now the Irish Volunteers also wanted rifles and live

[6] Jonathan Bardon, *A History of Ulster*, Belfast, 1992, p. 147

ammunition, especially as no attempt had been made to disarm the Ulster Volunteers. Erskine Childers, 30, a former clerk of the House of Commons and the author of an early example of a spy novel, *Riddle of the Sands*, which warned of the German naval menace in the North Sea, put together a plan. This Englishman, a passionate supporter of Home Rule, sailed his yacht *Asgard* to Hamburg, bought arms there and began the voyage back to Ireland.

PRONI- T2125/3/27

Erskine Childers

Mary Spring Rice and Mrs Erskine Childers on board *Asgard*

On Sunday 26th July 1914 the rifles were unloaded at Howth in full daylight. Scuffles with British troops followed when some weapons were shouldered by Volunteers marching to Dublin city. Then along one of the Liffey quays, soldiers opened fire on a taunting crowd,

Getty Images 3261251

Irish Volunteers training on Dublin rooftop with arms.

killing four people and wounding a further thirty-seven. Nationalists concluded that they had been treated very differently from Northern Unionists. Though another yacht landed more weapons unseen on the lonely Wicklow beach of Kilcoole, these weapons were antiquated single-shot Mausers loaded with black powder cartridges and there were not very many of them.

Asquith made ever more frantic attempts to push the Irish problem to one side. King George V was so alarmed by the situation that he intervened personally. He called an all-party conference at Buckingham Palace on 21st July and said in his opening address: 'To me it is unthinkable, as it must be to you, that we should be brought to the brink of fratricidal strife upon issues apparently so capable of adjustment as those you are now asked to consider, if handled in a spirit of generous compromise'. The conference, according to Churchill, 'toiled around the muddy byways of Fermanagh and Tyrone', as party leaders argued whether any, some, or all of Ulster's nine counties should or could be excluded by partition from Home Rule.[7] There was no 'spirit of generous compromise' and the talks broke down on 24th July.

---

[7] Buckland, *Irish Unionism: Two, Dublin and New York*, 1973, p.99; Stewart, 1967, p. 229

'I see no hopes of peace...we shall have once more to assert the manhood of our race'

Archduke Franz Ferdinand

Archduke Franz Ferdinand, heir-apparent of the Austro-Hungarian Empire, paid an official state visit to Sarajevo, the capital of Bosnia, on his wedding anniversary, 28th June 1914. The former Turkish province of Bosnia had been formally annexed by Austria-Hungary back in 1908: this had been to the fury of neighbouring Serbia, a state which felt that this province should be an integral part of its national territory. The Archduke's visit was certainly provocative: it was made on St Vitus's Day, the festival of Serbia's national patron saint. If, for example, during the darkest days of Northern Ireland's late twentieth-century Troubles the Prince of Wales had made a visit to Crossmaglen on 9th August, the anniversary of the imposition of internment in 1971, it could hardly have been more ill-advised than this rash imperial journey to Bosnia. In any case, Austrian security in Sarajevo was extraordinarily lax. Three Serb students, aspiring assassins, lay in wait. Their first assassination attempt led to some entourage being wounded, but the intended victims were unscathed. Only when the Archduke decided to visit the injured in hospital, and the imperial motor car drove down a street where the conspirators were discussing their failure, did an opportunity for a second attempt occur. One of them, Gavrilo Princip, was able to jump on the running board and shoot both the Archduke and his wife dead.

Illustration by Achille Beltrame in an Italian paper, *Domenica del Corriere*, depicting Gavrilo Princip killing Archduke Franz Ferdinand of Austria in Sarajevo.

When news of the assassinations in Sarajevo reached Britain and Ireland, very few thought it would result in a general European war. Certainly the Prime Minister did not. Asquith for years had been preoccupied with domestic issues including widespread labour disputes and direct action by suffragettes seeking votes for women – Ulster suffragettes in early 1914 burned down Major-General Sir Hugh McCalmont's home in Whiteabbey, at a cost of £11,000, and, in Belfast, Orlands House, the Tea House at Bellevue, Annadale Hall, and the pavilion of the Cavehill Bowling and Tennis Club were also burnt.[8] But Ireland remained Asquith's main anxiety. The island was lurching closer to the brink of civil war. In Ulster the danger was most acute where the nationalist Irish Volunteers – 41,000 in the province out of a national total of 129,000 – and loyalist Ulster Volunteers could be seen drilling in adjacent streets.

PRONI – INF/7/A/3/42

UVF on parade in 1913.

The Prime Minister would have been even more worried had he known that key positions on the Irish Volunteers' executive were held by militants of the secret Irish Republican Brotherhood. One of them, Tom Clarke, 34, the former dynamiter from Dungannon released from penal servitude, would be the principal organiser of the Easter Rising of 1916. Early in 1914 Clarke wrote to a fellow Tyrone republican organiser in Philadelphia, Joe McGarrity:

---

[8] Brett, *The Buildings of Belfast 1700–1914*, London, 1967, p. 63

Tom Clarke
Irish Republican Brotherhood

> *Joe, it is worth living in Ireland these times – there is an awakening... Wait till they get their fist clutching the steel barrel of a business rifle and then Irish instincts and Irish manhood can be relied upon.*

Shortly afterwards, as it became obvious that compromise on Home Rule was not possible, Sir Edward Carson gloomily observed:

> *I see no hopes of peace. I see nothing but darkness and shadows... we shall have once more to assert the manhood of our race.* [9]

Carson meant Ireland. Little did he know that the manhood of his race would be asserted, not in his homeland but in Flanders fields, the Somme, Gallipoli, Salonika, Palestine and at sea in the most terrible conflict the world had yet seen.

---

[9] F X Martin in F X Martin and F J Byrne (eds), *The Scholar Revolutionary: Eoin Mac Neill*, Shannon, 1973, p. 171; A T Q Stewart, 1967, p. 223

Chapter 2 WAR DECLARED – VOLUNTEERS MARCHING TOGETHER?

'The one bright spot in the very dreadful situation'

Sir Edward Grey, British Foreign Secretary.

The British Foreign Secretary, Sir Edward Grey, though distinctly unenthusiastic about Home Rule, loved Ireland and wrote elegantly about the superb fly fishing for trout available there. He was slow to recognise the seriousness of the situation following the assassinations of the Austrian Archduke and his wife in Sarajevo. Grey tended to let the Balkan crisis slip to the end of the cabinet agenda after Ireland had been, once more, debated at length. Like the Prime Minister, Grey liked to spend the weekends away from London, free from business, even during July 1914. Asquith also allowed himself a great deal of free time, in particular to write long letters to a young lady, Venetia Stanley, with whom the sixty-two-year-old Prime Minister was obsessively in love.

Conrad von Hötzendorf, Chief of Staff of the Austro-Hungarian armies, was determined to smash Serbian nationalism once and for all, almost regardless of the consequences. The assassination of the Archduke provided a unique opportunity to do so, he repeatedly said to his aged Emperor, Franz Josefis – Britain would be disabled by the Ulster crisis and would be unable to interfere to any effect. In Berlin General von Bernhardi assured his colleagues that the critical situation in Ireland would paralyse Britain 'if it ever comes to war with England'. The American ambassador to the German Empire

Conrad von Hötzendorff, 28th May 1916.

General von Bernhardi, 1910.

reported to Washington that it was 'believed by the Germans that Ireland would rise in rebellion the moment war was declared'.[10]

Kaiser Wilhelm II, 1915.

Theobald von Bethmann Hollweg

Conrad got the war he had long sought. On 5th July Kaiser Wilhelm II of Germany and his Chancellor, Theobald von Bethmann Hollweg, told the Austrians to take a strong line with Serbia and, above all, if Russia threatened to support Serbia, Franz Josefis could be sure of German military backing (later known as the 'blank cheque'). The Austrians, even though they found no proof that

---

[10] A T Q Stewart, 1967, p. 227

had received direct support from the government in Belgrade, presented an ultimatum to Serbia on 23rd July. On 25th July Serbia accepted most though not all of the demands. It was not enough. On 28th July Austria-Hungary declared war on Serbia.

Why was this war not limited to the Balkans? Europe had become divided into two armed camps. On the one side there was the Triple Alliance composed of Germany, Austria-Hungary and Italy; and on the other the Triple Entente made up of France, the Russian Empire

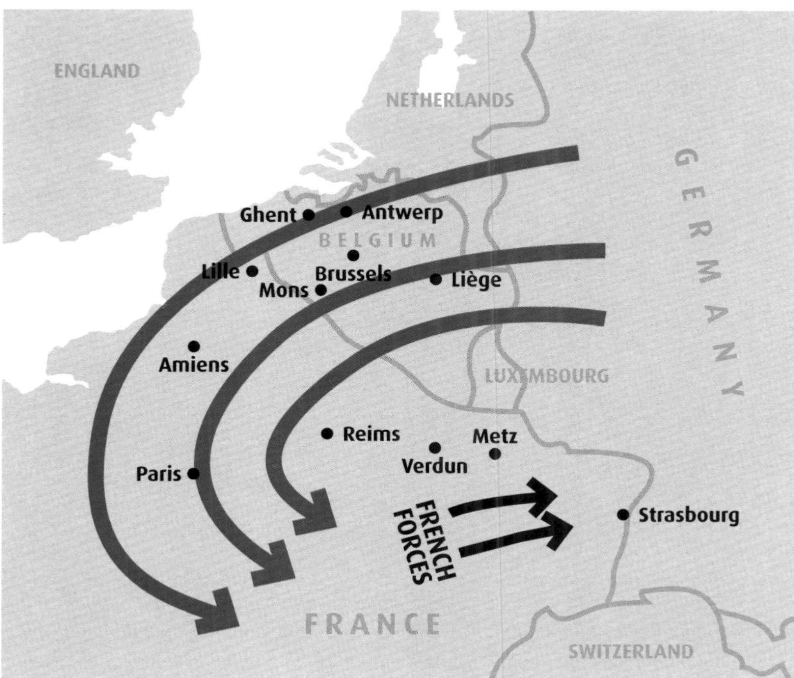

The revised Schlieffen Plan

Tsar Nicholas II of Russia

and Britain. Nicholas II, Tsar of Russia, ordered his huge army to mobilise, to make ready for war. As soon as Russian soldiers began to pull on their boots, however, there was panic in the German imperial court. The Schlieffen Plan had been devised for just such an event: to avoid a long wasting war on two fronts, the German high command had prepared a scheme to make a swift assault westwards through neutral Belgium, knock France out of the war, and then turn east to meet the 'Russian steamroller'. Now it appeared that the Tsar's army could be taking Berlin while the Germans were still approaching Paris. The generals were convinced that there could be no delay. 'Willy be a man!', his wife Augusta Victoria said to the Kaiser when he hesitated momentarily. The necessary orders were signed.

And so the Germans by the third day of August 1914 had declared war not only on Russia but also on its ally France. The Kaiser's war machine was the first to lurch into action and soon German troops were pouring into Luxembourg and Belgium. Britain, like Germany, had signed a treaty long before guaranteeing Belgian neutrality.

This 1839 treaty had now been torn up by the Kaiser and his government. Asquith and his ministers had an agonising decision to make. Churchill was keenest to declare war; Lloyd George was the most reluctant; Grey made it clear that he had promised to help France; and Asquith got his government to send an ultimatum to Berlin.

PRONI - INF/7/A/2/3

Sketch of Sir Edward Carson leader of the Ulster Unionists.

On the evening of 3rd August 1914 Sir Edward Grey addressed a hushed House of Commons. An ultimatum had been sent from London to Berlin to demand Germany's withdrawal from Belgium: this would expire at midnight. On that emotional night both Redmond and Carson pulled back their followers from the brink of civil war. 'I say to the Government that they may tomorrow withdraw every one of their troops from Ireland', Redmond said in the House to his fellow MPs, '...the armed Catholics in the South will only be too glad to join arms with the armed Protestant Ulstermen'. Carson, who was not present, later sent a telegram: 'All officers, non-commissioned officers and men who are in the Ulster Volunteer Force...are requested to answer immediately his Majesty's call, as our first duty as loyal subjects is to the King'. With evident relief Grey said that night that 'the one bright spot in the very dreadful situation is Ireland'. No doubt Asquith shared this sentiment as he realised that, in Churchill's words, 'the parishes of Fermanagh and Tyrone faded back into the mists and squalls of Ireland'. [12]

Even in the United Kingdom agreement to fight had been made in the cabinet room and the British Government had already ordered army mobilisation when Grey rose to speak in the Commons on 3rd August.

'Bless the good fortune which brings us together'

It was understandable that German commanders tended to think that Britain's entry into the war would make little difference. Britannia certainly ruled the waves with the world's largest navy, which had been absorbing one quarter of government expenditure

[12] Michael Laffan, *The Partition of Ireland 1911–1925*, Dundalk, 1983, p. 46; Jonathan Bardon, 1982, p. 183

each year, but as the Kaiser laughingly said to his generals: 'Dreadnoughts have no wheels!' [13] Unlike the United Kingdom all the continental powers had huge conscript armies. When fully mobilised the armies of the Russian Empire numbered five million. The German Empire fielded over three million; France over two million; and Austria-Hungary around two million. Britain's regular army, including reserves, made up entirely of volunteers, numbered no more than 400,000 – this was even smaller than Serbia's which totalled around 420,000.

The Anglo-Irish aristocracy and gentry made up an extraordinarily high proportion of commissioned officers in the British Army. These men have with some justification been compared with the Junkers, the landed gentry of Prussia, who supplied an exceptionally large number of Germany's commanding officers. Sir John French from a landed family in Co. Roscommon, was put in charge of the British Expeditionary Force. Henry Wilson, his second-in-command, came from Currygrane in Co.Longford. The newly-appointed Secretary of State for War, Field Marshal Horatio Kitchener, was born in Ballylongford, Co. Kerry. All these men were implacably opposed to Home Rule for Ireland.

Sir John French

PRONI-INF/7/A/3/158

Henry Wilson

Based on secret talks with the French for years beforehand, the British Expeditionary Force (BEF) was to be shipped across the Channel and take its place beside the French. As the Germans forged their way through Belgium, British troops – however few in number – would be needed to join their ally in the defence of Paris. The first

[13] Max Hastings, *Catastrophe: Europe goes to war 1914*, London, 2013,

task was to call up both the regular troops on leave and all reservists to join their Colours ready to be taken to France and Belgium. As an experienced commander brought back from retirement, Kitchener was already concluding that this war would not be over by Christmas. For the time being, mass conscription was out of the question. Thus, as the regulars were preparing for immediate action, Kitchener, with the full support of Asquith's government, prepared to put into effect a plan to raise a great army of volunteers, and train and equip them, so that Britain would have an army which would match those of the other great powers. During August 1914 the War Office authorised the formation of six 'New Army' divisions, and more would follow.

Throughout the nineteenth century Ireland had been a fruitful recruiting ground. At one stage, in the 1830s, more than half of all the soldiers in the British Army were Irish. Some counties, such as Carlow, Kilkenny and Mayo, had a strong tradition of young men seeking a career in the armed forces. The socialist republican and ex-soldier, James Connolly, called this 'economic conscription' and, indeed, it was true that poor employment prospects in the countryside helped recruitment. In 1900 the song at the top of the hit parade was 'What do you think of the Irish now?', an acknowledgement of the contribution Irish regiments had made in the Boer War, as are the monuments to the Irish who fell in that conflict: the bronze statue of a soldier with a fixed bayonet on the east side of Belfast City Hall; and the great memorial arch in St Stephen's Green in Dublin.
Some reservists had joined either the Ulster Volunteers or the Irish Volunteers. Now they got their call-up papers. The response of the people was extraordinarily good natured considering that only a very short time before Ulster was threatened with civil war. *The Irish News* reported that as early as 5th August

> *About six hundred men attached to the Irish Volunteers in Belfast were called up, and there was a great gathering to wish them God-speed…while at the same time a quota of the Ulster Volunteers were being "seen off" by a cheering crowd with a band and pipers.*

In the euphoria, traditional enmities were suspended, and the following day this verse – composed jointly by a Belfast member of

COPY OF MESSAGE.

"Please tell all Irishmen from me how
"deeply interested I am in their present effort
"to increase the Irish Forces in the Army. Born
"and brought up in Ireland as I was, I feel
"certain that my Countrymen will not allow our
"brave Irish soldiers to feel that they are
"unsupported by those at home.

"We ought not to see our Irish Divisions and
"Regiments kept up to strength in the field by
"other than Irishmen.

"Such neglect on our part would be a deep
"disgrace to Ireland. They MUST be Irish to a
"man.

"I appeal for men from Ireland on behalf of
"those gallant men in the Irish Regiments, our
"Regiments, who have fought so magnificently."

Yours very truly,

Kitchener

Message from Kitchener to Irishmen

the Ulster Volunteers and an Irish Volunteer from the Glens of Antrim – was published in the same newspaper:

> Bless the good fortune which brings us together,
> Rich men and poor men, short men and tall;
> Some from the seaside and some from the heather,
> Townsmen and countrymen, Irishmen all;
> Ulstermen, Munstermen, Connachtmen, Leinstermen,
> Faithful to Erin, we answer her call!

This doggerel, of course, would not achieve the fame of Rupert Brooke's 'Now God be thanked Who has matched us with His hour', but it was written in the same spirit. On Monday 10th August, *The Irish News* carried this report from Omagh:

'TYRONE'S FINE EXAMPLE. NATIONAL AND ULSTER VOLUNTEERS MARCH TOGETHER. ROUSING SCENES'

The Ulster Volunteers and Irish National Volunteers united at Omagh on Friday night in giving a most hearty send-off to the final draft of the Army Reserve of the Royal Inniskillings, who left the town about half-past nine o'clock, and a scene of unparalleled description was witnessed when the procession of both bodies of Volunteers and military marched through the town together…Subsequently, as both bodies of Volunteers paraded the town, they met one another and respectfully saluted.

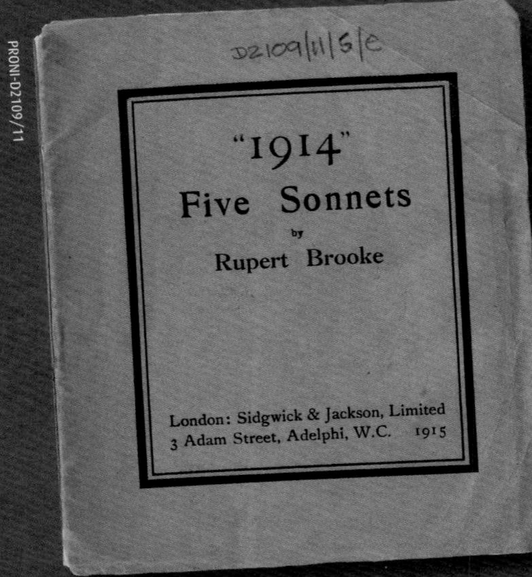

Book of Rupert Brooke's poetry

There was a similar scene in Strabane next day at the end of which Captain Roderick Gallaher of the Irish Volunteers 'called for three cheers for the Ulster Volunteers, the call being responded to in a most spirited manner'. Captain William Smyth of the Ulster Volunteers in turn called for a rousing three cheers for the Irish Volunteers.[14]

---

[14] *Irish News,* 6 and 10 August 1914

Chapter 3 WITH THE BRITISH EXPEDITIONARY FORCE IN FRANCE AND BELGIUM

Meeting 'a force of nature like a landslide'

General Aleksandr Samsonov

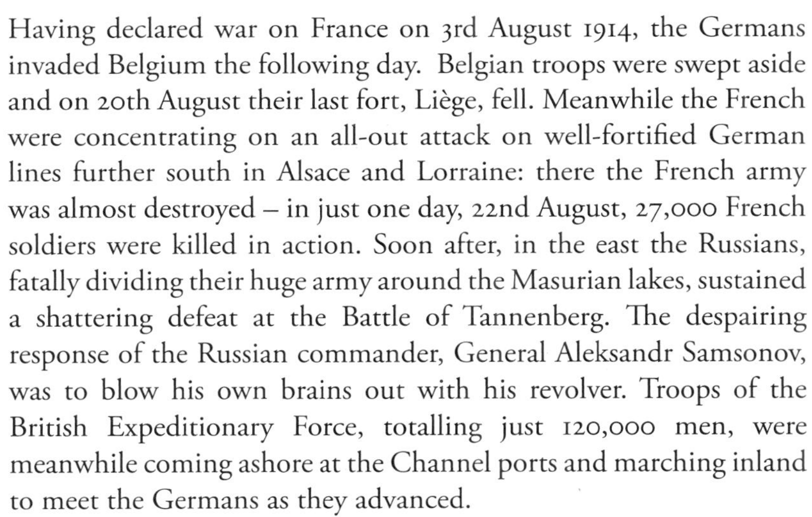

Having declared war on France on 3rd August 1914, the Germans invaded Belgium the following day. Belgian troops were swept aside and on 20th August their last fort, Liège, fell. Meanwhile the French were concentrating on an all-out attack on well-fortified German lines further south in Alsace and Lorraine: there the French army was almost destroyed – in just one day, 22nd August, 27,000 French soldiers were killed in action. Soon after, in the east the Russians, fatally dividing their huge army around the Masurian lakes, sustained a shattering defeat at the Battle of Tannenberg. The despairing response of the Russian commander, General Aleksandr Samsonov, was to blow his own brains out with his revolver. Troops of the British Expeditionary Force, totalling just 120,000 men, were meanwhile coming ashore at the Channel ports and marching inland to meet the Germans as they advanced.

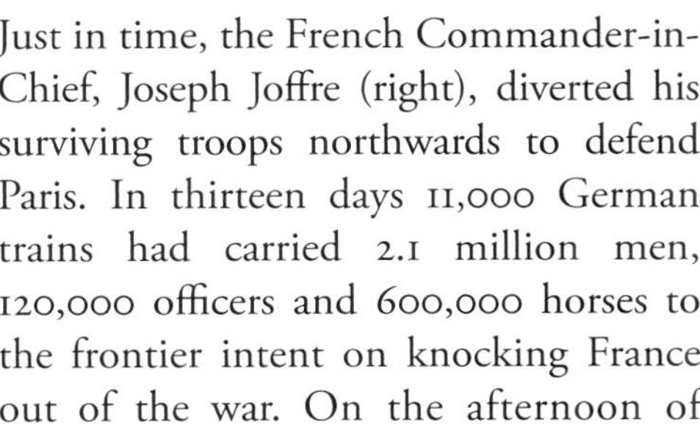

Just in time, the French Commander-in-Chief, Joseph Joffre (right), diverted his surviving troops northwards to defend Paris. In thirteen days 11,000 German trains had carried 2.1 million men, 120,000 officers and 600,000 horses to the frontier intent on knocking France out of the war. On the afternoon of

22nd August the Germans triumphantly entered Brussels. Harding Davis, an American journalist, watched them: 'No longer was it regiments of men marching, but something uncanny, inhuman, a force of nature like a landslide, a tidal wave or lava sweeping down a mountain'.[19] That same morning, thirty-five miles south of Brussels, the British entered the mining town of Mons right in the path of this German lava flow. Here the very first British shots in the ground war were fired by a squadron of the 4th Royal Irish Dragoon Guards.

Regular battalions of three Ulster infantry units – 2nd Royal Inniskilling Fusiliers, 2nd Royal Irish Rifles and 1st Royal Irish Fusiliers – were in the thick of the fighting at this stage and were to suffer heavy casualties.

---

[19] Max Hastings, 2013, p. 181 and p. 202

PRONI – D2966/121/12

Signal Section Royal Irish Rifles

Royal Inniskillings badge

Silk postcard to Cpl Hamilton 1st Battalion The Royal Irish Rifles

Discharge papers for John Doran who served in the Royal Irish Rifles.

A high proportion of these Ulstermen were from west Belfast and it is striking that these were Catholics and Protestants in the same units fighting together. A very lucky few would survive the war. One was a reservist of the 2nd Inniskillings, Private Andrew McCormick of Emerson Street in the Shankill. He had joined up in 1897, had served in the Boer War and after that in Crete, Malta and North China. By November 1918 McCormick, now a company sergeant-major, had earned the Distinguished Conduct Medal and the Russian Medal of St George (third class). Others were not so fortunate. Corporal Michael McGivern, a reservist in the 2nd Royal Irish Rifles who had been employed in Greeves's flax-spinning mill and had joined the Irish Volunteers, was killed in action less than a fortnight after arriving in France. His unit had acquired the label, 'West Belfast Battalion'. Father Henry Gill, the battalion's Jesuit chaplain, wrote later: 'About seventy per cent of the men of the 2nd R. Irish Rifles were Catholics, chiefly from the North of Ireland, but with a large sprinkling from the other parts of the Province'. [20]

Most BEF soldiers were veterans and their rapid and accurate rifle fire inflicted serious losses on the enemy. But they were overwhelmingly outnumbered: Sir John French had no choice but to order them to pull back. At le Cateau the BEF again halted briefly, slowed down the German advance, and after suffering heavy casualties retreated once more. The French army offered much more formidable resistance but, first the Belgians and then the BEF, had in a small way given crucial time for French forces to form up in front of Paris to defend it. Then, on the 5 September 1914, the French halted the Germans along the River Marne. Over the next ten days the exhausted Germans pulled back to the River Aisne. The modified Schlieffen Plan

[20] Richard Grayson, 2009, pp 23–37

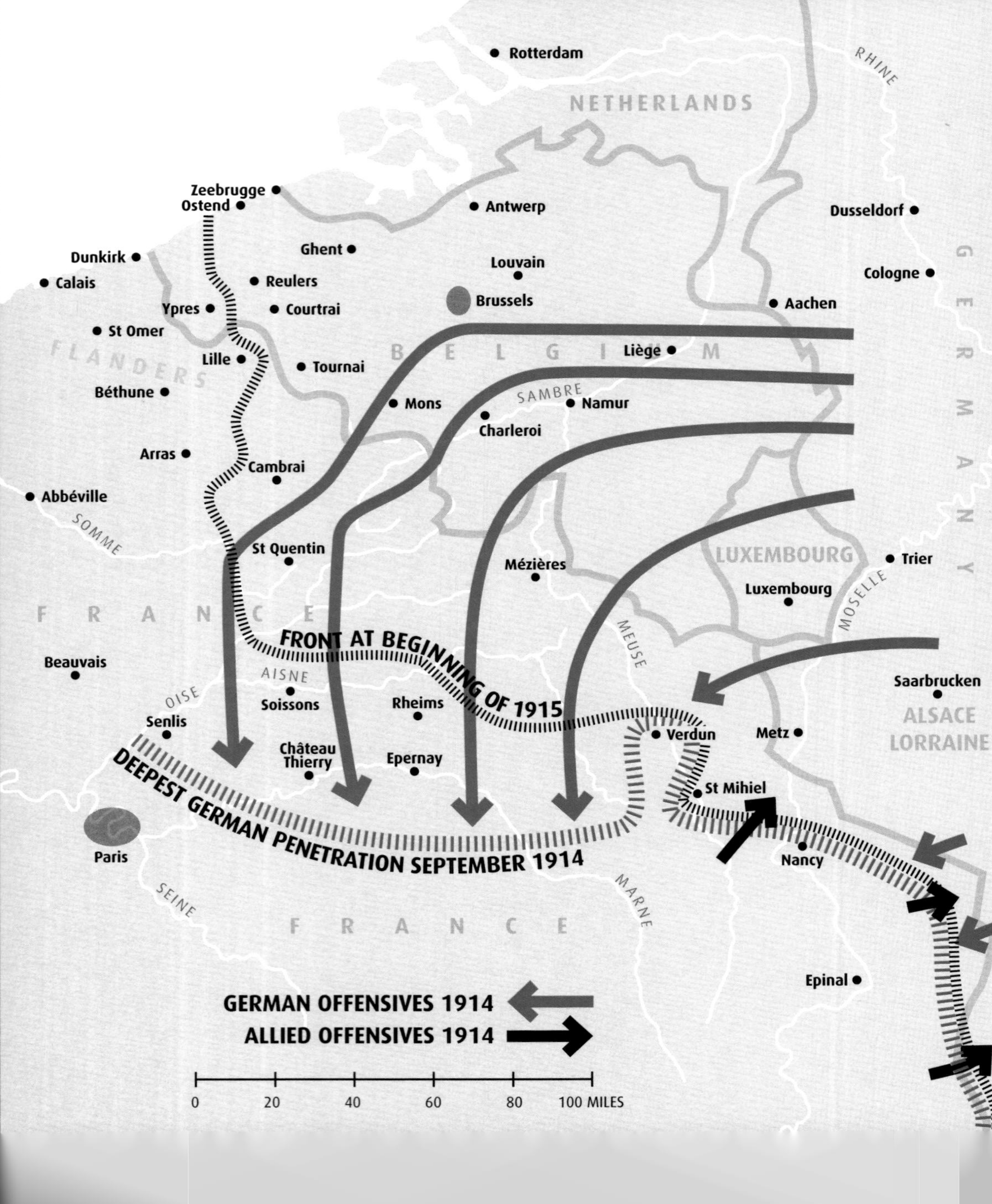

Rotterdam
RHINE
NETHERLANDS
Zeebrugge
Ostend
Antwerp
Dusseldorf
Ghent
Dunkirk
Louvain
Calais
Reulers
Cologne
Ypres
Courtrai
Brussels
Aachen
St Omer
FLANDERS
Lille
Tournai
BELGIUM
Liège
Béthune
Mons
SAMBRE
Namur
Charleroi
Arras
Cambrai
Abbéville
SOMME
GERMANY
St Quentin
Mézières
LUXEMBOURG
Trier
Luxembourg
MOSELLE
FRANCE
MEUSE
FRONT AT BEGINNING OF 1915
Beauvais
AISNE
Saarbrucken
OISE
Soissons
Rheims
ALSACE LORRAINE
Senlis
Verdun
Metz
Château Thierry
Epernay
DEEPEST GERMAN PENETRATION SEPTEMBER 1914
St Mihiel
Paris
Nancy
SEINE
MARNE
FRANCE
Epinal
GERMAN OFFENSIVES 1914
ALLIED OFFENSIVES 1914
0
20
40
60
80
100 MILES

had failed. Unable to go any further the Germans began to dig trenches for the first time. Facing relentless fire, the equally exhausted Allied troops advancing towards them, halted and began to dig trenches themselves.

Royal Ulster Rifles Museum

Three of the British Campaign medals: The *1914 Star, British War Medal* and the *Victory Medal.*

Often referred to as the *Mons Star* the *1914 Star* (left) was sanctioned in 1917 for members of the British Expeditionary Force for services during the first phase of the war. It was issued to those who served under fire in France and Belgium between 5th August 1914 and 22nd November 1914. This award is incomplete without the *British War Medal* and *Victory Medal*, as these two awards were automatically issued to those with the star.

Over the ensuing weeks and months lines of trenches stretched out until they extended along this Western Front from Switzerland to the North Sea. Though less continuous, trenches also ran from the Baltic Sea south to Romania and eventually to the Black Sea in what became known as the Eastern Front. In the west, at any rate, the war of movement was over. Over the next months and years the war developed into an inconclusive and bloody slogging match with no victory in sight for either side.

The BEF had performed poorly at the Marne but, sent north-west, it fought fiercely at Ypres in October, helping to keep a small slice of Belgium in Allied hands. By December 1914 this expeditionary force had lost 16,200 officers and men killed, 47,707 wounded, and 16,746 missing or taken prisoner. The United Kingdom desperately needed the service of the great new armies of volunteers now in training and still recruiting.

Royal Irish Rifles Camp on parade at Randalstown.

Reproduced with kind permission of the Doran Family and the Imperial War Museum.

William Porter Royal Irish Rifles (pictured with his wife Molly) died at Vierstraat on 17th May 1915, having survived the Battle of Mons. He left behind a young son, named William Mons Porter, pictured here after the war wearing his father's 1914 Star.

E
114275
1

No. 8552. Act. Corporal William Porter,

2nd Bn. Royal Irish Rifles.

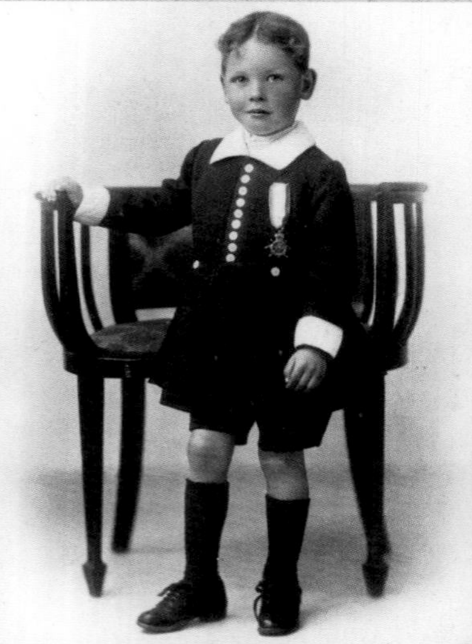

E/114275/1

In the Event of my
Death I give Everything
To the Above Mention

Signed By
Rfm. W. Porter
A. Coy. Roy. Ir. Rifles

In the Event of my Death I give
All I Possess to My Wife

Mrs. Wm Porter
C/o Mrs. Hamilton
off Antrim Road
Whitewell
Belfast

Signed By
Corpl. Wm. Porter
A. Coy. 2 Batt
Royal. Ir. Rifles
Expeditionary Force
8-3-15.

William Porter's will

Chapter 4 RECRUITING AND TRAINING VOLUNTEERS

'Have YOU any women-folk worth defending? Remember the Women of Belgium. JOIN TO-DAY'

All over Britain and Ireland recruiting posters festooned gable walls and hoardings. Conscription was not introduced into England, Wales and Scotland until 1916 and, though the attempt was made in the spring of 1918, conscription was never imposed in practice in Ireland. In short all those who joined up in Ireland, north and south, were volunteers. Why did so many willingly put their lives in danger? Some joined up because they came from families which traditionally made the army a career choice. The sudden closing of the Baltic as the war began cut Ulster off from its essential supplies of Russian flax. As a result many men as well as a great many women lost their employment in the linen mills and chose to take 'the King's shilling'. Undoubtedly most of the recruits had no idea how terrible and protracted the war would be.

Historians of the war have been struck by the importance given to patriotic duty by those joining. There is little doubt that the unprovoked invasion of neutral Belgium and the brutal treatment subsequently meted out to its citizens did much to help prospective recruits to make up their minds. Wild stories circulated about German soldiers raping nuns and bayoneting babies; these were unfounded but there is no doubt that the Germans displayed much brutality in Belgium during the first months of the war.

Army recruitment poster styled as a football match-day programme for "the greatest Match the world has ever seen".

GRAND
International Match

Great Britain, Ireland & Allies
Versus
Germany, Austria & Allies

Where Match will be Played:

SOMEWHERE IN GERMANY

Teams:

Unlimited number of players on each side

Referee:

UNITED STATES

Linesmen:

ITALY and HOLLAND

Irishmen wishing to play in this—the greatest Match the world has ever seen—**should enter their names at once** at the nearest Recruiting Office so that they may be thoroughly trained for the Great Day.

Medals will be presented after the Match.

(3265.) Wt.P.621— .50,000.3/15. ALEX. THOM & Co., Ltd., Dublin.

PRONI – LA/20/50/GA/5

The Germans were obsessed that some civilians were firing back at them and murdered civilians in retaliation – 10 in the village of Bernau on 4th August including family of five hiding in a cellar. One German brigade shot 117 civilians between 4th and 7th August. On 6th August 200 civilians were used as a human shield. On 8th August infantrymen herded 72 inhabitants of Melen into a field, including eight women and four girls under thirteen, and shot them dead. By that date 850 unarmed civilians had been murdered around Liège by German forces. A wounded Irish soldier in Dover hospital described to Asquith how he had witnessed Germans driving a shield of women and children in front of their advancing soldiers. On the night of 25th/26th August soldiers broke into the University of Louvain (mainly founded by Ulster Gaelic lords and Franciscans in the early seventeenth century) and burned it, destroying 300,000 volumes in the library. They also shot priests, academics and many unarmed civilians and destroyed 2,000 buildings by fire. Around 10,000 inhabitants were driven from the town and 1,500 were deported to Germany. By the end of the year 6,427 Belgian civilians had been murdered by the invading Germans.

Long before the full truth of these horrors became general knowledge, reference to German 'beastliness' played a central role in the publicity campaign to persuade men to join up. 'IRISHMEN! Remember Belgium. ENLIST NOW and DEFEND YOURSELVES', one poster proclaimed, showing a German wearing a spiked helmet, holding a rifle with blood dripping from his bayonet, with his foot on the body of a girl, her doll beside her. The poster exhorted volunteers to 'join the Irish Army Corps today…Your place is on the Battlefield and no true Irishman should be sought or found elsewhere'. Another poster proclaimed:

> Fight for Ireland! Remember Belgium! Have YOU any women-folk worth defending? Remember the Women of Belgium. JOIN TO-DAY.

Some propaganda went as far as urging Irishmen to fight for 'little Catholic Belgium' and much of the energy of the recruiting drive was directed at Redmond's followers. Indeed, Redmond's face adorned a recruiting poster which exhorted:

THE HUNS
HAVE DESECRATED & DESTROYED THE
CATHEDRALS OF FRANCE & BELGIUM
IRISHMEN DO YOUR DUTY!
ENLIST & KEEP THE ENEMY OUT

Have You any
women-folk worth
defending?
Remember
the Women of
Belgium
JOIN TO-DAY
HELY'S LIMITED, LITHO. DUBLIN. P661.

RALLY ROUND THE FLAG
"WE MUST HAVE MORE MEN"
Copyright Design THE PUBLICITY ARTS LONDON
Apply, RECRUITING OFFICE,
BALLYMONEY, CO ANTRIM, IRELAND.

Your first duty is to take your part in ending the war. Join an Irish regiment to-day.

Other posters proclaimed: 'I'll go too! The real Irish spirit!' and another showing a bugler, with the words, 'THE CALL TO ARMS: IRISHMEN DON'T YOU HEAR IT?

Reference to German barbarism of course was also effective in persuading loyalists to join up. The appeal to patriotic duty to serve King and country was powerful. Posters which appeared all over Ulster included:

> What in the end will settle this war?
> TRAINED MEN
> It is YOUR DUTY to become ONE

and

> BRITAIN is FIGHTING for the FREEDOM of EUROPE
> and to DEFEND YOUR MOTHERS, WIVES AND
> SISTERS FROM THE HORRORS OF WAR –
> ENLIST NOW

Another poster, 'Rally round the Flag' showed the flags of the Allies encircling the Union flag including the flag of the Empire of Japan which had declared war on Germany on 23rd September 1914.

On Monday 11th August a large advertisement proclaiming 'Your King and Country Needs You' appeared for the first time in the *Belfast Newsletter*. A similar one had appeared the day before in *The Irish News*. At first there seemed to be some difference of opinion amongst loyalists about joining up. On 7th August an 'elderly volunteer' had written that a recruiting drive was about to be launched, asking Ulster Volunteers 'if they are willing to serve abroad…It is highly probable that many of them will never return. When the war is finished, and the Home Rule situation has to be faced again, the UVF will be without many of its most useful members, and as a fighting force it will be less formidable.

Your King and Country Need You.

A CALL TO ARMS.

An addition of 100,000 men to his Majesty's Regular Army is immediately necessary in the present grave National Emergency.

Lord Kitchener is confident that this appeal will be at once responded to by all those who have the safety of our Empire at heart.

TERMS OF SERVICE.

General Service for a period of 3 years or until the war is concluded.

Age of Enlistment between 19 and 30.

HOW TO JOIN.

Full information can be obtained at any Post Office in the Kingdom or at any Military depot.

GOD SAVE THE KING!

Belfast Newsletter Saturday 8th August 1914

WHAT IN THE END WILL SETTLE THE WAR?
TRAINED MEN
IT IS YOUR DUTY TO BECOME ONE.

Recruitment poster

BELUM.0429.1973 Photograph © National Museums Northern Ireland
Collection Ulster Museum

Therefore I ask you, is it desirable that any Volunteer should offer himself for foreign service?' Others argued to the contrary: 'our men will be thoroughly trained, if necessity arises, to fight for our liberties, later on'. Several prominent men hoped that what they had said in the recent past would be forgotten. Captain James Craig, for example, had said in January 1911 that if the people of Ulster were put out of the Union, he 'would infinitely prefer to change his allegiance right over to the Emperor of Germany'.

'my mother was crying all the time': joining up

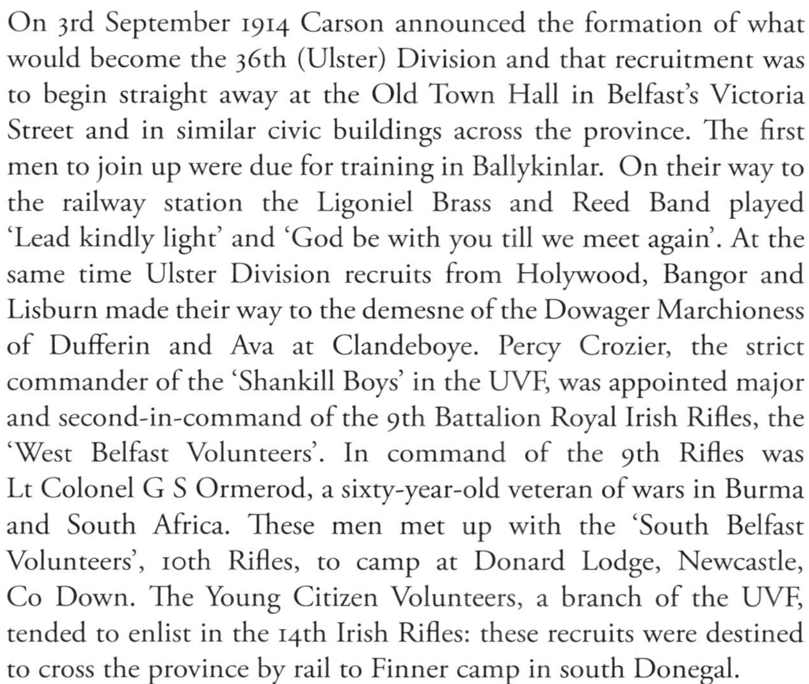

On 3rd September 1914 Carson announced the formation of what would become the 36th (Ulster) Division and that recruitment was to begin straight away at the Old Town Hall in Belfast's Victoria Street and in similar civic buildings across the province. The first men to join up were due for training in Ballykinlar. On their way to the railway station the Ligoniel Brass and Reed Band played 'Lead kindly light' and 'God be with you till we meet again'. At the same time Ulster Division recruits from Holywood, Bangor and Lisburn made their way to the demesne of the Dowager Marchioness of Dufferin and Ava at Clandeboye. Percy Crozier, the strict commander of the 'Shankill Boys' in the UVF, was appointed major and second-in-command of the 9th Battalion Royal Irish Rifles, the 'West Belfast Volunteers'. In command of the 9th Rifles was Lt Colonel G S Ormerod, a sixty-year-old veteran of wars in Burma and South Africa. These men met up with the 'South Belfast Volunteers', 10th Rifles, to camp at Donard Lodge, Newcastle, Co Down. The Young Citizen Volunteers, a branch of the UVF, tended to enlist in the 14th Irish Rifles: these recruits were destined to cross the province by rail to Finner camp in south Donegal.

The Ulster Division recruitment tramcar as it appeared in the *Belfast Evening Telegraph* on February 23rd 1915. The tram traversed all routes in Belfast from 9am until 10pm with three recruiting officers on board, conveyed recruits to the Old Town Hall in Belfast for enlistment daily. The car was illuminated after nightfall, presenting a very striking appearance as it moved through the streets of Belfast.

Many of those seeking to join up lied about their age. David Bell, aged 37 and captain of the UVF company in Ballynahinch, said he was 34 and nine months (the upper age limit was 35). The lower legal limit was 19; some under-age recruits were fetched back by parents but many others were recruited without difficulty. Recruitment was slower in the countryside, partly because early autumn was perhaps the busiest time of the farming year. One boy, then living in Mill Street, Lurgan, recalled:

> *We walked to the station, and my mother was crying all the time...I remember my father telling my mother to dry her tears for he would be back in next to no time...On the platform I saw Father squeeze my mother's hand and give her a sort of kiss... It was lonely that night without my father.*[23]

Apart from a few in the 14th Royal Irish Rifles, Catholics, understandably, were almost completely absent from the 36th (Ulster) Division. In the north the desire of nationalists to join up was just as strong as it was for unionists, even after the Woodenbridge speech – but where would these volunteers go? Kitchener's announcement on 12th September that the 16th Division was to be an Irish one was a great relief for Redmond. General Sir Lawrence Parsons was appointed to command the new division. The Irish Party leader's faithful lieutenant in Ulster was Joseph Devlin. 'Wee Joe', who had begun his career as a bartender, then became a talented journalist, and ousted Henry Henry, the Catholic Bishop of Down and Connor, from control of the Irish Party machine in Belfast. In 1907 he won West Belfast for the Nationalists by a margin of sixteen votes. At Westminster, he soon acquired the nickname, 'the Pocket Demosthenes'. Devlin also revived the Ancient Order of Hibernians (a Catholic mirror image of the Orange Order) which had 60,000 members by 1909 (a great many of them in mid-Ulster). Now Devlin threw himself enthusiastically into persuading the National Volunteers to fight for King and Country.

For example, at a meeting in St Mary's Hall in Belfast on 4th October, Devlin called on the Volunteers to 'take their stand behind Mr Redmond'. What is particularly interesting is that the packed crowd not only sang 'God Save Ireland' and 'A Nation Once Again' but also 'God Save the King'. At that stage it was reckoned that around a thousand of Redmond's volunteers in the city had joined up. The rate of Catholic recruitment in Belfast

[23] Philip Orr, 1987, pp 48–52

increased in the late autumn as the strongly-unionist *Belfast Evening Telegraph* admitted on 12th November; 'during the week efforts have been made by some local Nationalists to get their men to join the army'. A cohort of 60 men had met at the National Club in Berry Street and then enlisted in Clifton Street and more were to follow. Lord Basil Blackwood, a passionate opponent of Home Rule, wrote to his mother, the Dowager Marchioness of Dufferin and Ava, about Devlin's recruiting zeal:

> *In one respect you would find Devlin congenial company. In spite of stories about his drunkenness, he is a rigid teetotaller. He is also very keen about recruiting and General Parsons wrote to him the other day to say he was the only man who got them recruits, so you see every Devil has a silver lining.* [24]

The 36th (Ulster) Division was able to keep units of the UVF, often with their officers, almost intact. Transferred to the British army, they continued to drill with the same men from the same districts as before. In addition, most were receiving training in camps not too far distant from their homes. Irish National Volunteers, however, often found themselves separated from their friends (serving, for example, with the Connaught Rangers and the Royal Dublin Fusiliers) and sent for training at the other end of the island. A great many were summoned to the camp at Fermoy in Co Cork.

WELCOME AT FERMOY.

Northern Recruits Escorted to the Barracks.

Great enthusiasm prevailed at Fermoy last night, when the second contingent of the Belfast National Volunteer recruits for the Irish Brigade arrived by special train. They were met at the station by representative townsmen, including the chairman of the Urban District Council (Mr. E. J. Quinlan, J.P.), who, on behalf of the townspeople, gave the men a hearty welcome. Several military officers of the Fermoy garrison were in attendance to take charge of the arrangements. On alighting, the contingent lined up, and were marched out to the music of several bands and pipers of the Leinster Regiment. Outside the station a great concourse of townspeople had assembled, and they greeted the new recruits with whole-hearted warmth. A de-

The Irish News 26th November 1914 describes troops arriving at Fermoy Camp in Co. Cork.

On 19th November 1914 around 600 Irish National Volunteers who had joined up were given a warm send off from Belfast. Singing Irish military songs they marched behind 'pipers in Gaelic costume, flourishing banners emblazoned with the Red Hand of the O'Neill and distinctively Irish devices and mottoes'. As they reached the Great Northern Railway terminus in Great Victoria Street, 'God Save the King' was sung along with the 'war song' of the football club, Belfast Celtic. Joseph Devlin said farewell to each man individually before the train set off for Dublin and on

---

[24] Richard Grayson, 2009, p. 14; Public Record Office of Northern Ireland D/1231/K/10/1-16

to Co Cork. At Fermoy, the Belfast men were greeted by bands and met by local Irish National Volunteers. The northern and southern volunteers paraded together at the Volunteer Drill Hall in Fermoy before being escorted to their camp. Another 350 recruits left Belfast for Fermoy on 25th November and when they arrived, the Irish News observed, 'everywhere the sharp Northern accent was heard'. That newspaper's correspondent reckoned that eighty per cent of the National Volunteers in Belfast had joined up. The divisional commander, General Parsons, wrote to Redmond to inform him that 'We are getting good batches of I.N.V. from Ulster & have already filled the 6th Connaught Rangers'.

A good many of these were experienced veterans. They included 62 year-old John McManus from Majorca Street in Belfast who was immediately appointed company sergeant-major in the 18th Royal Irish Rifles. Originally from Leitrim, Co. Down, he had enlisted in 1889 and served in the Far East, the Mediterranean, and the Boer War. Daniel McKeown, from the Springfield Road, since he was also a Boer War veteran, was given the task of training men of the 5th Royal Irish Fusiliers in the 10th (Irish) Division. Francis McCann of McDonnell Street, wounded in the Boer War at Tegula Heights, trained soldiers of the 8th Royal Irish Fusiliers in the 16th (Irish) Division. [25]

'You must steel your hearts and minds... That is war': training for action

The time allotted for training recruits varied widely. Men from the 10th Division saw action long before those of the 16th and 36th Divisions. Sending the New Army divisions into battle was a huge logistical operation which required the production of small arms, artillery, shells, canteen equipment, medical supplies and other requirements of total war. Foot drill formed a core element of the training provided. The men were taught 'personal administration', that is, to take proper care of weapons, uniforms and equipment.

[25] Richard Grayson, 2009, pp 15–20

The British Army had a well-deserved reputation for its high-quality musketry drill and, as far as possible, the men were given regular practice to promote skill at arms. Shortage of ammunition at this stage was a serious problem, however, and some men in the Ulster Division complained of the poor quality of many of the cartridges provided. It is difficult to avoid the impression that much of the training was not particularly useful: a good deal of energy was expended in simply making sure that the recruits were fit and kept busy. Private David Starrett, 9th Battalion, Royal Irish Rifles, observed:

> *Ballykinlar was a dismal hole, nothing but sandhills hemmed in by Dundrum bay…But it was in that dismal hole our boys were really trained to be one of the best fighting brigades in France.*[26]

PRONI – INF/7/A/3/92

Ulster Division being inspected at Ballykinlar 1914

Major-General C H Powell, commander of the 36th (Ulster) Division, a keen climber who had ascended peaks in the Caucasus and Himalayas, emphasised the importance of physical training through long route marches. Since equipment had still to arrive, the men marched with rucksacks filled with stones or shipyard rivets. Much time was spent in drilling and bayonet practice. One lad, still too young to join up, recalled seeing training in progress at Clandeboye. He would wander towards the camp and, through a gap in the hedge, watch the troops training:

[26] William Sheehan, *The Western Front: Irish Voices from the Great War*, Dublin, 2011, p. 6

> *There was drill with rifles, marching, squads doing PT [physical training], bayonet fighting, stabbing at stuffed figures suspended from a sack...there were high wire frames over which men hurled grenades like tossing a cricket ball.*

One of the main problems in the 36th Division was absence without leave because training camps were so close to the homes of recruits. Captain Percy Crozier, found that his 107 Brigade – also known as the 'Belfast Brigade' – contained many tough characters. His recipe was severe discipline. To ensure that his men would prove to be formidable on the battlefield this eccentric martinet did his best to promote 'blood-lust'. Over six months he lectured his junior officers five nights a week explaining at length just how they should prepare themselves to shed the blood of the enemy. Lt Colonel Spencer Chichester advised his staff: 'You must lose your gentle selves. You must steel your hearts and minds and be callous of life and death. That is war'.

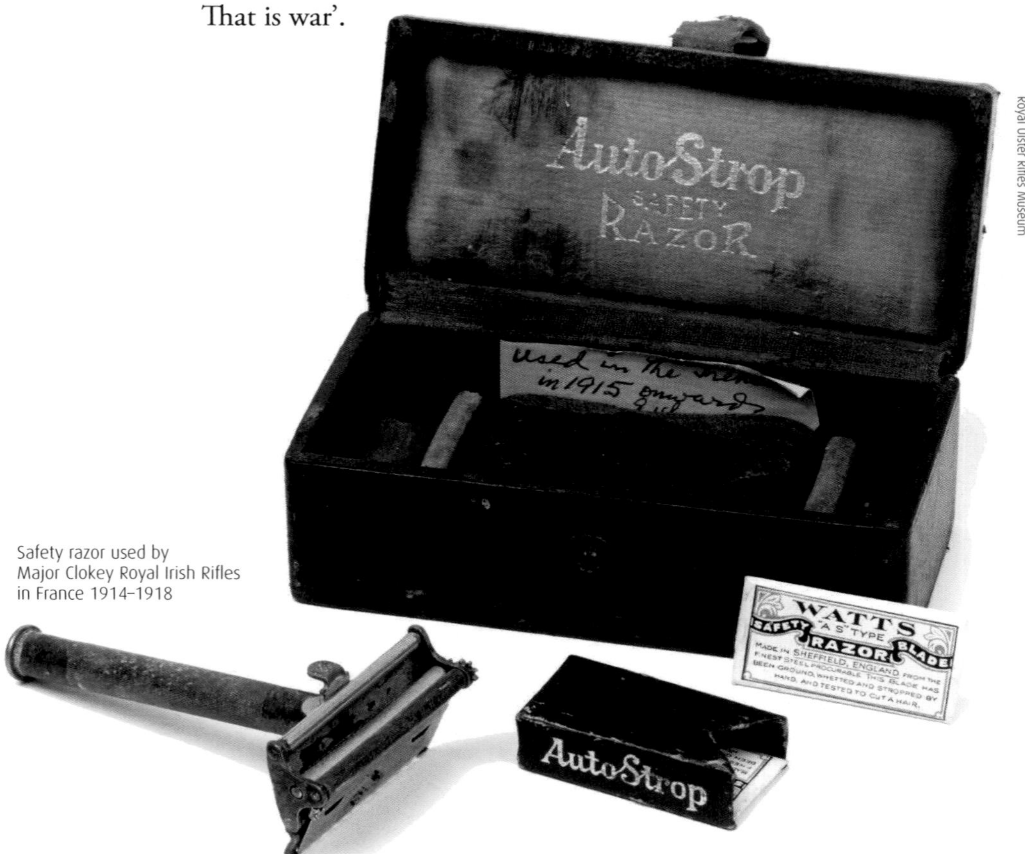

Royal Ulster Rifles Museum

Safety razor used by Major Clokey Royal Irish Rifles in France 1914–1918

The camp routine involved: rising at 6 a.m.; first parade at 7 a.m., followed by exercises and an obstacle course; 8 a.m. breakfast of bread butter and tea, usually with cheese, or tinned salmon or sardines; a long parade from 9 a.m. to 12.30; 1 p.m. lunch, generally of soup, beef and potatoes; another parade from 2 p.m. to 4.30 p.m., followed by tea. A good deal of rest time was absorbed by cleaning uniforms and equipment. During the final months men were taught how to 'entrain', that is, how to board and get off a train in an orderly fashion. Rows of seats were laid out in a field to represent a carriage, and the men would be marched out in companies to perfect the process.[27]

By the late spring of 1915 the Ulster Division was ready to leave. On 8th May 17,000 men, the entire division, were inspected at Malone

36th (Ulster) Division arriving at review at Malone 8th May 1915.

PRONI - INF/7/A/3/96

PRONI - INF/7/A/3/101

36th (Ulster) Division review at Malone.

with Major General Sir Hugh McCalmont taking the salute and Major General C H Powell on his right. At 1.15 p.m. the troops marched to Belfast city centre; at 2.30 p.m. Sir Edward and Lady Carson stood with the Lord Mayor at the City Hall; at 2.45 p.m. Powell and his senior officers were in the van; then followed the cavalry of the Inniskilling Dragoons, the Cyclists Company wheeling their cycles, four field companies of engineers, the signals company, pontoon and field equipment, and infantry brigades led by 107 infantry brigade. The Co. Down Volunteers, playing

[27] Philip Orr, 1987, pp 54, 59 and 66; Richard Grayson, 2009, pp 17–18

PRONI – INF/7/A/3/106

36th (Ulster) Division review at Malone, troops receiving rations.

36th (Ulster) Division marches past Belfast City Hall, 8th May 1915 Field Ambulance Convoy.

PRONI – INF/7/A/3/112

36th (Ulster) Division marches past Belfast City Hall, 8th May 1915.

PRONI– INF/7/A/3/116

'The Mountains of Mourne' on their fifes and drums, attracted enthusiastic applause from the thousands packed together to bid them farewell. The parade had been arranged in part to encourage further recruitment and posters along the route asked

PRONI – D2026/1

S4/127946
WILL.
30/9/15
In the event of my death
I leave the whole of my
property and effects
To Mrs Wm Kane
Bridge St
Kilrea
Co L-Derry Ireland
Pte George W Kane
A S C
S/4 127946

Will of Private G.W.Kane
3rd Field Bakery Army Service Corps
c.1915–1917.

> *Wouldn't you rather be marching with your pals to-day than looking on?*

and

> *Is the Ulster Division to be kept at home because you hesitate?*

The parade ended with the passing of over a hundred horse-drawn wagons of the Army Service Corps, the butchers and bakers, and finally the Royal Army Medical Corps, with its field ambulances. The crowd then sang the National Anthem.

The 16th Division was taken to Aldershot in September. The men of the Ulster Division were sent to Seaford in Sussex for further training. Kitchener inspected the division on 27th July and, rather late in the day, the troops were to be given musketry training at Bordon and Bramshott – up to now the shortage of ammunition meant that most men had hardly fired a shot. Powell, consoled with a knighthood and sent off to Vladivostock in charge of the Red Cross, was replaced by Major General Sir Oliver Nugent, who had already been in the thick of the fighting in France.

During the first days of October the men of the Ulster Division were taken across the Channel by a variety of transport vessels, including an Isle of Man paddle-steamer, to France.[28]

[28] Philip Orr, 1987, pp 76–77, and pp 83–84; Richard Grayson, p. 22

PRONI – D3394/3

Major General Oliver S.W. Nugent

Chapter 5 1915: ULSTER FORCES IN GALLIPOLI

The Turkish Empire closes the Straits

All this time, the soil of continental Europe was being soaked in blood as never before in its history. The events of August 1914 had proved that, given the military technology of the time, attack was not the best form of defence. Troops dug into trenches and shell-holes and protected by barbed wire were able, with machinegun fire, to inflict appalling casualties on men ordered 'over the top' and charging with fixed bayonets across no-man's land. Later, tanks and aircraft would restore advantage to the frontal assault but, until the last months of the war, defence was the best form of defence. Yet commanders on both sides persisted in the belief that they could 'break through' and march rapidly either to Berlin or Paris. Very few men of the original BEF now survived: in repeated futile offensives on the Western Front many more Ulstermen died in action – the numbers of Irish fallen, however, were dwarfed by the tens of thousands of Germans and French who every month paid the ultimate price. And yet more tens of thousands were dying in Serbia, Galicia and east Prussia.

In 1915 the Germans deployed a new weapon, poison gas: though the consequences of its use were horrific, gas was too difficult to control to make a serious difference. And, naturally, the Allies responded with their own poison gas. The 'Great War' was now becoming a world war. The Turkish Empire joined Germany and Austria-Hungary in October 1914. Romania joined the Allies, so Bulgaria joined the other side. Italy did not stick with the Triple Alliance and in May 1915 joined the Allies. And the number of states joining in the conflict continued to grow.

Turkey's entry into the war caused the Allies acute anxiety. Especially during the winter when its Baltic Sea ports were frozen over, Russia was isolated and not only her navy at Odessa and Sevastopol but also her merchant vessels were trapped in the Black Sea. In December 1914 the Grand Duke Nicholas, commanding the Russian army, made an impassioned appeal for help. Kitchener was sympathetic – as the former military master of Egypt he feared the Turks might seize the Suez Canal. But the most enthusiastic advocate of action against Turkey was the First Lord of the Admiralty, Winston Churchill.

Landing on the Gallipoli Peninsula

The plan was to launch a surprise attack from Egypt north to the straits separating the eastern Mediterranean from the Black Sea. The objective was to take Constantinople (now Istanbul) and open up the narrow waters to enable the western Allies to bring aid into

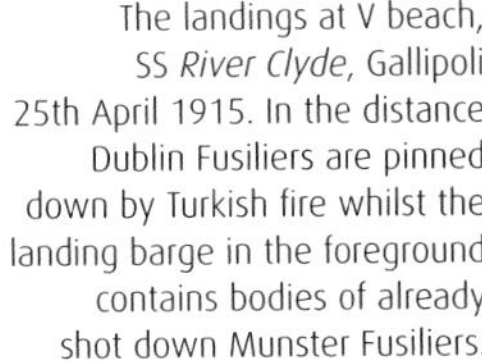

The landings at V beach, SS *River Clyde*, Gallipoli 25th April 1915. In the distance Dublin Fusiliers are pinned down by Turkish fire whilst the landing barge in the foreground contains bodies of already shot down Munster Fusiliers.

IWM – Q50473

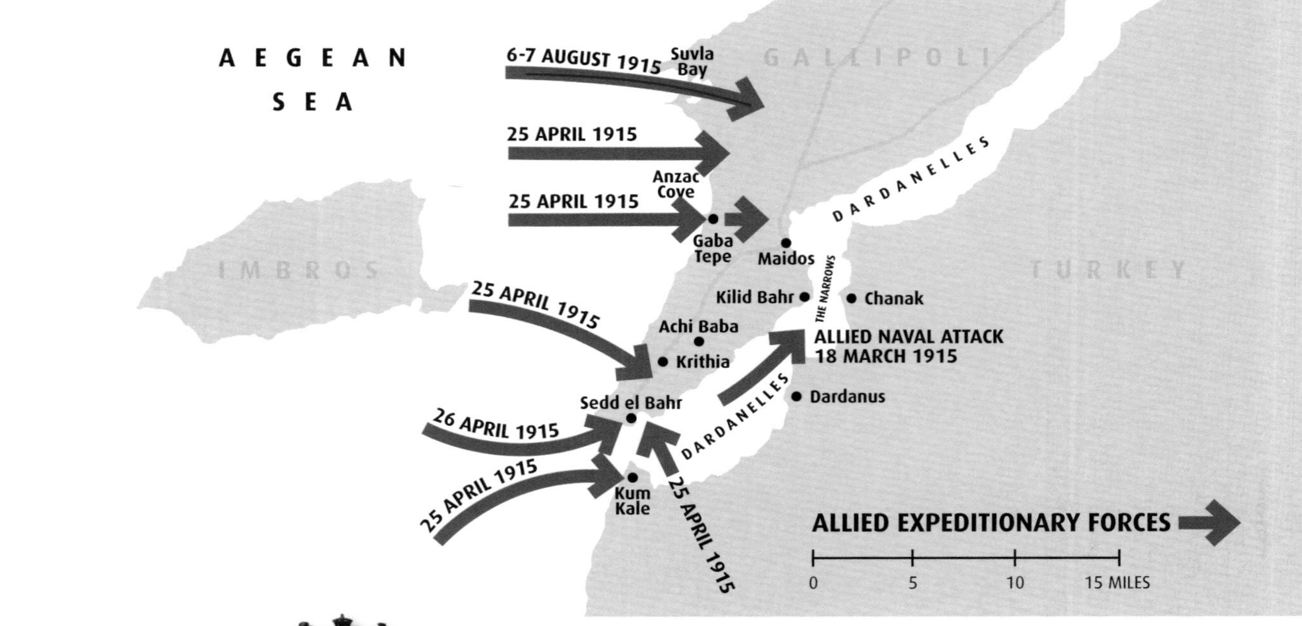

Illustration of ANZAC Troops after Gallipoli.

the Black Sea to Russia. If the plan had been swiftly executed, it had some chance of success. The campaign, however, was blighted from the outset by poor planning, inaccurate maps, inadequate provisioning and poor direction. Above all, the element of surprise, essential for success, was lost again and again. After a naval attack on Turkish forts along the Dardanelles Straits, an amphibious landing was to be made by French, British, and Australian and New Zealand (ANZAC) troops on the Gallipoli Peninsula.

Cunard R.M.S. *Mauretania*

One of Kitchener's New Army divisions, the 10th (Irish), was committed to this operation. In the early summer of 1915 the Cunard liner *Mauretania*, painted in naval camouflage, steamed its way through the Straits of Gibraltar and on to the eastern Mediterranean. Most of the men in this 17,000 strong division were southern Irish but a great many were also northerners recruited for the most part from the Irish National Volunteers. The 29th Division was Britain's main contribution to the initial landings and this included the 1st Royal Inniskilling Fusiliers who were members of the 87 Brigade. Bad weather frustrated the 29th Division's attempt to make a

PRONI – D989/C/3/71

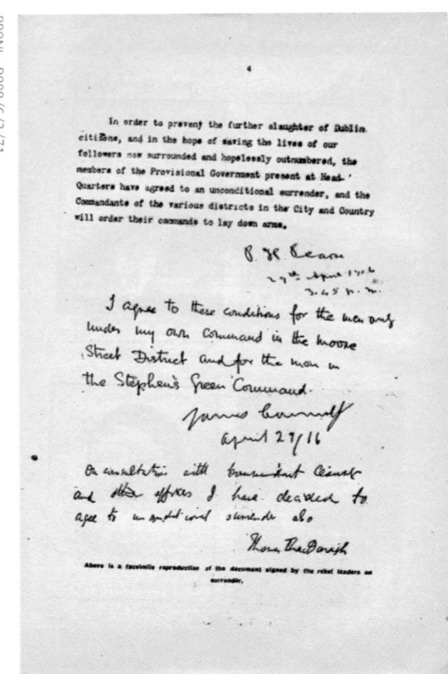

In order to prevent the further slaughter of Dublin citizens, and in the hope of saving the lives of our followers now surrounded and hopelessly outnumbered, the members of the Provisional Government present at Head-Quarters have agreed to an unconditional surrender, and the Commandants of the various districts in the City and Country will order their commands to lay down arms.

P. H. Pearse
29th April 1916
3.45 p.m.

I agree to these conditions for the men only under my own Command in the Moore Street District and for the men in the Stephen's Green Command.

James Connolly
April 29/16

On consultation with Commandant Ceannt and other officers I have decided to agree to unconditional surrender also

Thomas MacDonagh

Above is a facsimile reproduction of the document signed by the rebel leaders on surrender.

Declaration of surrender signed by P.H. Pearse, James Connolly and Thomas MacDonagh.

seized buildings in the centre of Dublin on Easter Monday 24th April. Many Irish Volunteers (those opposed to fighting with the British in the war) joined these insurgents. Though the Proclamation of the Republic claimed the support of 'gallant allies in Europe', a German attempt to bring rifles to Ireland had been foiled by the Royal Navy and IRB miscalculation. Numbering barely 2,000 men and boys, with virtually no effective support outside Dublin, and armed for the most part with antique Mauser rifles, this rebellion had no hope of military victory. Following heavy artillery bombardment on Sackville Street (now O'Connell Street), the insurgent commanders had no choice but to agree to an unconditional surrender. At least 450 people, many of them innocent civilians, had been killed; 2,600 had been wounded; and much of central Dublin had been reduced to rubble. This was at a time when over 145,000 Irishmen were engaged in a deadly conflict in the trenches.

IWM Q 90445

British troops man a street barricade in Dublin during the Easter Rising, 1916.

Martial law had been proclaimed and on Friday 28th April General Sir John Grenfell Maxwell arrived to take charge in Dublin. On 2nd May the first courts martial began. At dawn on 3rd May the first executions of leaders by firing squad took place in Kilmainham Gaol. Fifteen men had been executed by 12th May. Each execution, each one announced in a blaze of publicity, shocked the Irish public who had earlier condemned the rebellion. Even Carson declared: 'No true Irishman calls for vengeance'. He recognised that a whole new cohort of republican martyrs was being created. Nationalist opinion was now undergoing a seismic change.

On the Western Front, Tom Kettle, a former Nationalist MP, now a lieutenant in the Royal Dublin Fusiliers, received news of the insurrection in Dublin. In a letter home he gave his opinion of the insurgents: 'These men will go down in history as heroes and martyrs; and I will go down – if I go down at all – as a bloody British officer'.[32] Shortly afterwards Kettle found himself at the River Somme, ready to take part in a great offensive. Here Kitchener's New Army divisions joined the French along a front of eighteen miles, ready to take part in largest battle yet to be fought in this war.

1 July 1916: 'They went down in their hundreds'

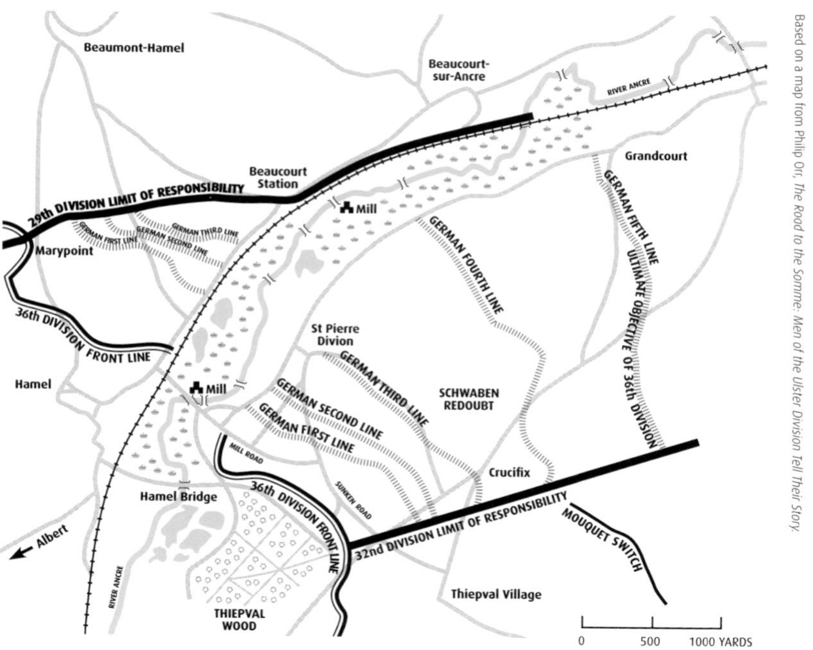

Based on a map from Philip Orr, *The Road to the Somme: Men of the Ulster Division Tell Their Story.*

The 36th (Ulster) Division's front line straddled the River Ancre, a tributary of the Somme. On the south side the front line stretched

[32] Keith Jeffery, *Ireland and the Great War*, Cambridge, 2000, p. 61

in front of Thiepval Wood. There the objective was to take the Schwaben Redoubt, a complex of trenches, fortified machine-gun posts and dugouts. Rising over 1,000 yards 250 feet above the Ulstermen, this fortification was protected by sixteen rows of barbed wire in front of the German first line and at least five in front of the second line. North of the Ancre the division was to cross a ravine and three lines of German trenches north of Hamel village to take Beaucourt railway station.

Just after dawn on 1st July 1916 the men readied themselves as the five-day Allied artillery barrage, the heaviest the world had ever seen, reached a horrific climax. 'As the shells passed over our heads', John Stewart-Moore observed, 'the air hummed like a swarm of a 100 million hornets'. Each man about to go over the top carried a great burden: in addition to a rifle, a waterproof sheet; a woollen waistcoat; two Mills grenades; 170 rounds of ammunition; two sandbags in their belts; two smoke helmets; goggles; and rations. Captain Percy Crozier was there with his men:

> *Jimmy Law comes round from Brigade with a chronometer to synchronise the time, as everything had to be done to the second…*
> *'Don't you go and get shot to-day, Jimmy; your mother would never forgive me'…*
> *The men fall in, in fours…A pin could be heard to drop.*[33]

Major General Sir Oliver Nugent, unlike most other divisional commanders, had decided to order his men into no-man's land before zero hour. This was to bring them closer to the German lines before the whistles were blown in the knowledge that the Ulstermen would be well protected by the final, intense Allied barrage. At 7.10 a.m. Armagh Volunteers left their trenches and lay down in no-man's land, waiting for the signal to attack. More men followed to join them at 7.20 and 7.30 a.m. South of the River Ancre men from South Antrim, Down, Tyrone and Derry crossed the parapet into no-man's land at 7.15 a.m.

---

[33] Philip Orr, 1987, p. 142, and pp 152–154

IWM – Q 53

Battle of the Somme. A support company of an assault battalion, of the Tyneside Irish Brigade, going forward shortly after zero hour on 1st July 1916 during the attack on la Boisselle.

At 7.30 a.m. officers blew their whistles and the men advanced further across no-man's land at a steady marching pace as instructed. It was the anniversary of the Battle of the Boyne; some men wore orange lilies and at least one sergeant draped his sash over his uniform. But the massive bombardment had neither cut the wire nor knocked out the German machine-gun nests. North of the Ancre the attack proved a disastrous failure: troops were caught by crossfire in a deep ravine. According to a survivor the bullets 'came like water from an immense hose with a perforated top'. One German soldier recalled: 'We just had to load and reload. They went down in their hundreds. You didn't have to aim, we just fired into them. If only they had run, they would have overwhelmed us.' Opposite Thiepval Wood, however, 109th Brigade, already part-way across no-man's land before zero hour, took the enemy completely off balance, capturing the Schwaben Redoubt and reaching the German fourth line where the fighting was like 'a Belfast riot on the top of Mount Vesuvius'. R H Stewart was close to 'as hard-faced, crooked a sergeant as ever walked on two feet' and recorded his exploits:

> *The old sergeant kept going till we reached the German lines. With the first bomb he threw the door off a deep dugout, and the next two he flung inside. He must have killed every German in it. We left him sitting just below the parapet with a grenade in each hand ready for the next live German that came along.*[34]

[34] Philip Orr, 1987, pp 167–168

In fact the Germans had excavated so deep into the soft porous chalk, constructing spiral stairways, that they had not only been well protected from the Allied shells but also, very often, from grenades thrown into their dugouts at close quarters. Some were able to emerge behind the advancing Ulstermen and fire on them.

Dangerously overextended, exposed to relentless fire and mistakenly shelled from their own side, whole companies disappeared. By nightfall all gains had been lost.

'Blacker's Boys' – men recruited from Armagh, Monaghan, and Cavan Ulster Volunteers – returned with only 64 out of 600 men who had gone over the top.[35] Seventeen-year-old Private Herbert Beattie wrote home to Belfast:

> *Dear Mother,*
>
> *Just to let you know I am safe and thank God for it for we had a ruf time of it in the charge we made. Mother, don't let on to V. Quinn mother or Archers mother they they must be killed wounded for they are missen of roll call, and tell Hugh the fellow that youst to run along with E. Ferguson called Eddie Mallin he youst to have Pigens if Hugh dus not no him McKeown nows him tell them he was killed, tell them ther is not another grosvenor Rd fellow left but myself. Mother wee were tramping over the dead i think there is onley about 4 hundred left out of about 13 hundered...Mother if god spers me to get home safe i will have something uful to tell you if hell is any wores i would not like to go to it Mother let me here from you soone as you can....*
>
> *This is all I can say at present from your loving son Herbie.*
>
> *Mother* ××××××××××××××××××
> *Father* ××××××××××××××××××
>
> *Show my Father this letter and tell him to writ*[36]

[35] Philip Orr, 1987, pp 167–173, and p. 181

[36] Private Beattie's letter transcribed for Jonathan Bardon by Kathleen Page in 1969

Emma Duffin, a volunteer nurse from Belfast and daughter of a Unionist MP, waited to treat the wounded at le Havre. She wrote in her diary:

> *I had not been on night duty very long when the big push began and the trains came and came, and the boats did not come fast enough, and we worked all night and came on duty again after breakfast and prayed and looked for the boats, especially the* Asturias *as she was the biggest. I was sent on duty on the station platform; if the hospital had not made me realize the war I realized it that night; under the big arc lights in the station lay stretchers 4 deep...at the end of the station were the walking cases; they were past walking, and the majority had lain down huddled together, their arms in slings, and their heads bound up, the mud from the trenches sticking to their clothes and the blood still caked on them. I was up and down all night feeling I was in a bad dream...attempting the hopeless task of trying to make men with their legs in splints a little more comfortable, feeling the pulses of the men who felt faint, rearranging a bandage that had slipped and watching for haemorrhages.*[37]

Emma Duffin deserves a prominent place in the roll of honour of twentieth-century Ulsterwomen who made a positive difference and should be remembered. She left a written record (in elegant longhand) of incalculable value which has had to wait a full century since the outbreak of the Great War before being published. The diaries she wrote, first as a volunteer nurse behind the lines in the First World War, and then as nursing commandant at Stranmillis Military Hospital in south Belfast during the Second World War, give a rather different perspective than those usually provided in the memoirs of fighting men.

Emma Duffin had a comfortable and privileged upbringing. She was the fourth of Adam and Maria Duffin's nine children. Her mother was granddaughter of Dr William Drennan, the founder of the radical Society of United Irishmen, inaugurated in 1791. Her father

[37] Public Record Office of Northern Ireland, D2109/13

PRONI – D1556/27/6/5

On the front. 22. 8th 1916

Madam.

Excuse me if I am writing to you with a pencil and on such a so bad paper. I am in trenches since a long times and I can't do better. I want to say to you how I am grateful and honoured by your letter, Madam and how I should be pleased to receive some news from Irelande and in English writing. I beg your pardon, I know it will be a lot of mistakes in my letter, I have been only seven months and half in England and since two years I did not speak one english word. Excuse me.

Thank you letter sent from the front 22nd August 1916.

PRONI – D2109/18/4

Emma Duffin - V.A.D.
Served 1915 - 1919
Egypt and France
Made an Assistant Nurse
"Mentioned in Despatches"

PRONI – D2109/6

CERTIFICATE OF IDENTIFICATION.

Y M C A

No. 1619 No. of Passport 270929

Name Sylvia Mary Duffin

Residence Dunowen
Belfast

Status Spinster

Nationality British

Issued at
74, South Audley Street, W.

Jeanne Malcolm
Hon. Secretary.
Princess Helena Victoria's Auxiliary.
Committee of Y.M.C.A.

Date 17.4.19

S. M. Duffin.

was a successful stockbroker in Belfast and a prominent Liberal Unionist. Like her seven sisters, Emma was educated at home with governesses before being sent at the age of sixteen to Cheltenham Ladies College. In 1911 she went to Pomerania in Germany as an au pair to improve her German – this fluency would prove valuable in a way she could never have predicted. She attended courses at the Belfast College of Art and was becoming known as a book illustrator when she applied to be a volunteer nurse.

When war broke out in 1914 the British Red Cross and the Order of St John pooled resources to organise members into Voluntary Aid Detachments. Voluntary Aid Detachment recruits (known as VADs) enlisted for periods of six months at a time and, after some weeks training in First Aid, were sent to work in military hospitals, rest stations, convalescent homes and medical supply centres. Emma was thirty-one when she applied to be a VAD in 1915. Her first posting was in Alexandria in Egypt where men wounded in Gallipoli were being evacuated for treatment. At the end of her six-month service she re-enlisted and from 1916 to the end of the war she was based in two hospitals in northern France.

Emma's diaries paint vivid pictures of the horrors of war as the maimed and dying arrived – sometimes in overwhelming numbers – from the front lines of the Western Front. Along with professional nursing and medical staff, VAD nurses shared the occupational hazard of contracting infectious diseases. Emma was laid low by infections on several occasions. She records how (criticised by colleagues) she befriended a wounded German soldier. He told her that his two brothers had been killed in action. He knew he was dying and said that this would be very hard on his mother. Next morning Emma found that he had died and noted: 'Poor old German mother'.

Later, Emma added this postscript to her First World War diaries:

> *We had seen great suffering but greater courage. We had learnt to take responsibility and to act on our own when required. We had learnt to be patient. To accommodate ourselves to*

different surroundings. We had learnt the value of comradeship and that barriers between classes could be ignored: an orderly could be a friend as well as an officer, a patient could be a brother. To me, some of those men are more real than those I met perhaps a week or so ago. I can never forget them, as many I know will remember me. I was their 'sister' in both senses.

With thanks to Trevor Parkhill who supplied the information and excerpts above from his book *The First World War Diaries of Emma Duffin, Belfast Voluntary Aid Detachment Nurse.*[38]

During the first day of the Battle of the Somme, the bloodiest day in the history of the British army, the United Kingdom sustained over 54,000 casualties, 21,000 of them killed or mortally wounded.

PRONI – INF/7/A/3/152

Thiepval Battlefield, France, 1921.

The Ulster Division suffered a loss of 5,700 killed or wounded. Of these, at least 2,000 had been killed in action. These figures do not include casualties of other Ulstermen serving in different units along the eighteen-mile battle front on the first day of the battle. For example, the 1st Inniskillings, just to the left of the Ulster Division, lost 228 killed and 265 wounded; and the 1st Royal Irish Rifles (predominantly from west Belfast), fighting at Ovilliers with 600 men, had 56 men killed in action and 348 men wounded.[39]

---

[38] Trevor Parkhill, *The First World War Diaries of Emma Duffin, Belfast Voluntary Aid Detachment Nurse*, Four Courts Press, 2014.

[39] Richard Grayson, 2009, p. 91

Autumn at the Somme: Guillemont and Ginchy

It was on Friday 7th July that newspapers in Ulster began to report a great loss of life at the Somme. Telegrams in small buff-coloured envelopes began to arrive. Lists of those killed, wounded or missing appeared in the newspapers. One man in Lurgan wrote to a friend:

> *There is hardly a house in Hill Street in which at least one member of the family has not been killed or wounded. It is terrible, terrible hard news to bear with equanimity, for however just and right a cause it may be, the death of so many young men leaves our land the poorer.*

The Somme Heritage Centre

Ronald Waterman served with the 12th Royal Irish Rifles. He was killed on 1st July 1916 at the Somme. The Somme Heritage Centre holds a collection of letters he wrote home to his sister Maggie. The last letter is dated 26th June 1916. The family were from Glencollier Street in North Belfast.

The Orange Order decided to suspend the usual 'Twelfth' celebrations. The lists got longer and by Monday 10th July the *Belfast Evening Telegraph* began printing letters from wounded men and letters of sympathy written by officers and chaplains. Politicians added their tributes, emphasising the heroic sacrifice of those loyal to King and country – Lt Colonel S W Blacker of the Armagh Volunteers observed in a letter to a friend on 14th July that there had 'been a lot of extravagant stuff written and published in the press, which is a great pity'.[40]

In fact the Battle of the Somme had only just begun. It raged on bloodily all through the summer into the autumn. The 16th (Irish) Division moved up to the Somme at the beginning of September. The first offensive was to attack German positions at Guillemont, about five miles south-west of Thiepval. Tom Kettle wrote:

> *We are moving up to-night into the Somme. The bombardment, destruction and bloodshed are beyond all imagination, nor did I ever think the valour of simple men could be quite as beautiful as that of my Dublin Fusiliers... The big guns are coughing and smacking their shells.*

[40] Orr, 1987, pp 194–197

3/7/16

My Dearest Mother

Your Loving & affectionate Son

John

Best Love & kisses

A letter written by John Doran to his mother on 3rd July, telling her how he was feeling, having survived the Somme.

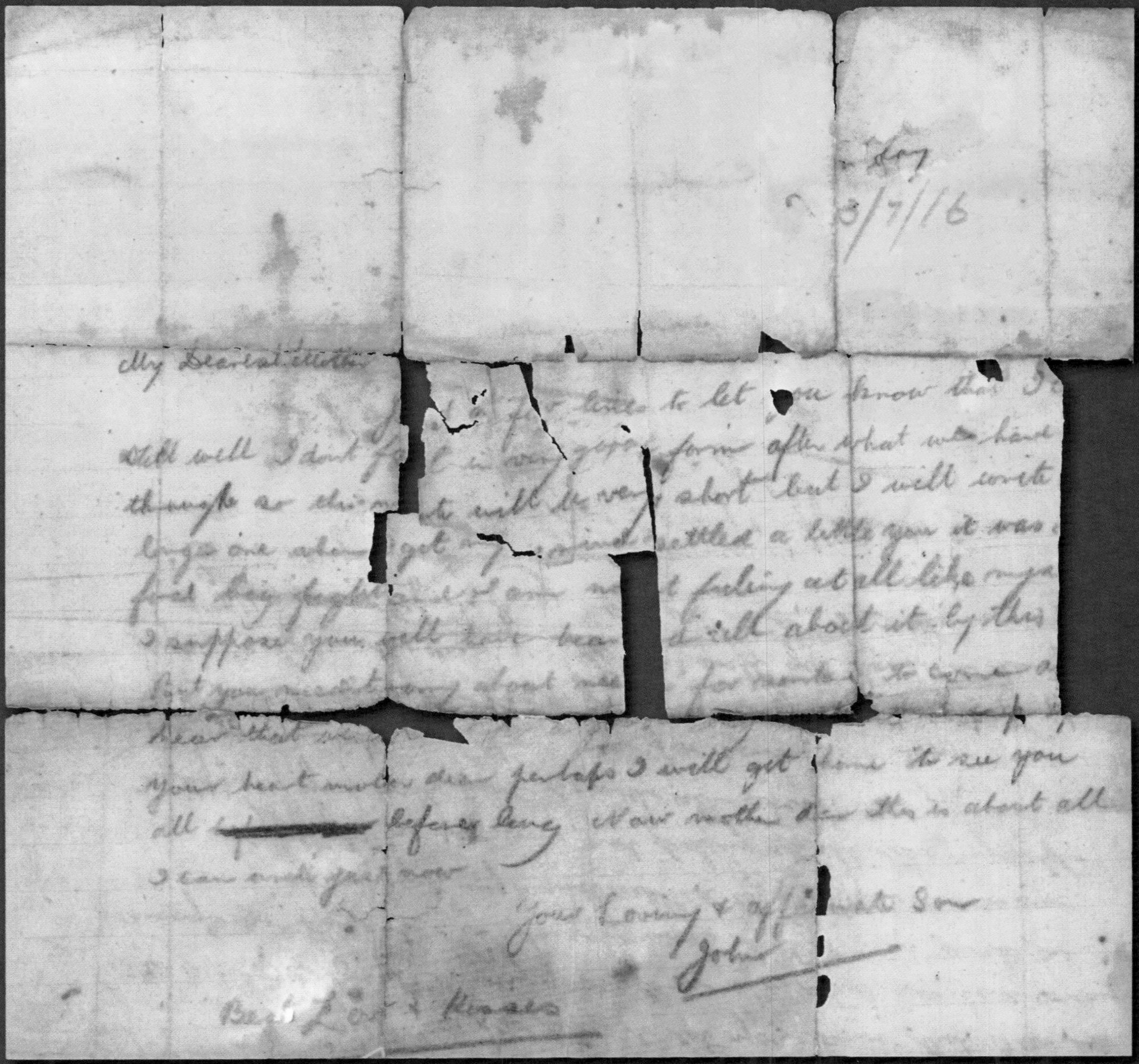

My Dearest Mother

Just a few lines to let you know that I am still well. I don't feel in very good form after what we have went through so this note will be very short but I will write a longer one when I get my mind settled a little. It was our first big fight and I am not feeling at all like myself. I suppose you will have heard all about it by this time, but you needn't worry about me…so keep up your heart mother dear perhaps I will get home to see you all before long. Now mother dear this is about all I can write just now.

Your Loving and affectionate Son

John

Best love and kisses

PRONI – INF/7/A/3/156

36th (Ulster) Division memorial. Lord Londonderry and Dr C F D'Arcy, Church of Ireland Archbishop of Armagh at the dedication of Thiepval Tower, Thiepval, 19 November 1921.

Days later Kettle was lying dead on the battlefield. The attack had begun badly, many men killed by 'friendly fire' as shells fired from heavy trench mortars behind them fell short amongst them. A second Allied offensive at Ginchy close by reaped another fearful harvest. Between 1st and 10th September 1916 the 16th (Irish) Division suffered 4,330 casualties of whom at least 1,079 lost their lives.[41]

It was not all disaster. Claud Potter commanded artillery south-west of Albert. On 14th September 1916 he recorded in his diary: 'Round Brigade HQs (122 and 124) in York Trench and visited dumps. Our guns giving the Hun a fine dose, his reply feeble. Saw the new Tanks. Hope they will be a great success'. He told his mother that the tanks (referred to by English soldiers as 'the Irish Navy') were like great whales. These slow-moving machines would eventually do much to turn the tide of war in the Allies' favour.

The protracted Somme offensive did in the end force the Germans to pull back to the Hindenburg Line – to some this was a sensible tactical retreat to a position of strength but to other Germans this was a signal that the Central Powers had lost all hope of victory. Allied losses had been so great however, that there is much truth in A J P Taylor's observation that 'idealism perished on the Somme'.[42]

---

[41] Terence Denman, *Ireland's Unknown Soldiers*, Dublin, 1992. p. 97; Richard Grayson, 2009, p. 98

[42] A J P Taylor, *The First World War: An Illustrated History*, London, 1963, p. 140

Chapter 7 THE HOME FRONT

An industrial and commercial powerhouse

No end to the fighting was in sight. It was now a war of attrition in which victory could only go to the side mobilising more men and harnessing the greater share of economic power. Ulster had made a crucial contribution to the United Kingdom's armed forces but it was also an arsenal of vital importance to the Allied cause.

The north-east of Ireland was then one of the planet's most dynamic corners. Ulster was the world centre of the linen industry. Back in 1895 Herbert Lanyon, president of the Belfast Chamber of Commerce, made this arresting speech:

Irish Linen Centre & Lisburn Museum Collection

> *I find the length of yarn produced in the year amounts to about 644,000,000 miles, making a thread which would encircle the world 25,000 times. If it could be used for a telephone wire it would give us six lines to the sun, and about 380 besides to the moon. The exports of linen in 1894 measures about 156,000 yards, which would make a girdle for the earth at the Equator three yards wide, or cover an area of 32,000 acres, or it would reach from end to end of the County of Down, one mile wide.*

Output was even greater in 1914. Entire towns, such as Gilford, Sion Mills and Drumaness, were devoted exclusively to processing flax into linen, though it was in Belfast by passing down the canyon

Irish Linen Centre & Lisburn Museum Collection

Advertising poster for Dunbar, McMaster & Co Ltd, linen thread manufacturers, Gilford, c 1900

of the Crumlin Road, flanked by tall forbidding mills, or by looking up at the great ornate warehouses of Donegall Square and Bedford Street, that the global dominance in this textile industry was made most obvious.

In January 1899 Harland and Wolff had launched from Queen's Island in Belfast the *Oceanic*, the largest man-made moving object ever constructed on earth in the nineteenth century and, indeed, up to that time and in ensuing years the company regularly built the largest ships in the world. Workman Clark, though popularly known as 'the wee yard', more than once launched a greater tonnage than any other shipyard on the globe.

Knocking off at Harland and Wolff, 1910. In the background huge gantries stand over slip No. 2, from which the *Olympic* has just been launched, and slip No.3, where *Titanic* nears completion

In 1900, after London and Liverpool, Belfast had been the port of third importance in the United Kingdom, then the greatest trading state on earth. Though Glasgow had by-passed Belfast in this respect when the RMS *Titanic* was launched at Queen's Island in 1911, Belfast on the eve of the Great War, still then Ireland's largest city, had the world's biggest linen mill, tobacco factory, linen machinery works, spiral-guided gasholders, tea machinery and fan-making works, aerated waters factory, dry dock, and handkerchief factory, in addition to the largest ship-building yard on earth.[43]

Tobacco and pipe gift box given to the 9th Battalion The Royal Irish Rifles. Manufactured by Murray Sons and Company Ltd in a factory which stood at the junction of Sandy Row, Hope Street and the Boyne Bridge in South Belfast.

Royal Ulster Rifles Museum

Coping with unrestricted submarine warfare

In the first couple of months of the war, Ulster's industrial production actually suffered some contraction. Linen, Ulster's biggest employer, had to cope with the cutting off of supplies of raw flax from Belgium

[43] Jonathan Bardon, *A History of Ireland in 250 Episodes*, 2008, pp 411–412

and the Russian Empire and it would take time for farmers to plough up the sward to grow this crop again as intensively as their forebears had done. In Belfast neither of the shipyards had any Admiralty work on hand in August 1914. Since the government gave priority to naval vessels, they were forced to cut back on their labour force – depleted by enlistment in any case – owing to the drop in orders for merchant and passenger ships. The workforce at Harland and Wolff fell by over 6,000 from 24,425 to 18,414 between the end of July and the end of October 1914.

Then, realising that this would not be a short war, Churchill, the First Lord of the Admiralty, ensured that orders flowed in. Skilled labour became so scarce that in the week ending 27th April 1915, 1,239 shipwrights and boilermakers each worked between sixty and eighty-five hours a week. By then Germany had launched a deadly campaign with its U-boats against Allied ocean-going commerce. The sinking of the *Lusitania* off the Old Head of Kinsale, Co Cork, on 7th May 1915 with the loss of nearly 1,200 lives – many of them American – threatened to bring the United States into the war, and for a time Germany moderated its U-boat campaign.

IRISHMEN
AVENGE THE LUSITANIA
JOIN AN IRISH REGIMENT
TO-DAY.

Survivors of the *Lusitania* at the Town Hall in Queenstown Co. Cork, May 1915. Enlistment posters are visible in the background.

Getty Images -3286472

Then early in 1917, the Kaiser's government threw caution to the winds and launched an 'unrestricted' submarine warfare sinking vessels on sight. The first high-profile victim was the SS *Laurentic*, sunk off Fanad Head, Co Donegal, with a loss of 354 lives. Completed at Queen's Island in 1909 as Harland and Wolff's first large passenger liner powered by marine turbines, the ship had been converted into an auxiliary cruiser. Most of the 43 tons of gold and silver on board was recovered after the war.

The Ulster Steamship Company, better known as the Head Line, sustained heavy losses. On 14th February 1917, just ten days after Germany had launched its campaign of unrestricted submarine warfare, the *Inishowen Head* was torpedoed off the Pembrokeshire coast. In March the company lost the *Bray Head*, followed in April by the *Howth Head*, *Torr Head* and *Dunmore Head* in a single week, the *Black Head* and *Bengore Head* in June, and the *White Head* and *Garron Head* in October and November 1917. With the loss of the *Glenarm Head* and the *Teelin Head* in January 1918, no fewer than 12 of the original 17 Head Line ships had been sunk, a total loss of 33,956 tons.

Information provided by Rorke Bryan, author of *Ordeal by Ice: Ships of the Antarctic* (Cork), 2011. His father George Bryan was third mate on the *Inishowen Head* and survived not only that sinking but also another torpedo attack in the Second World War.

Britain was now in peril. In April 1917 the U-boats sank 555,056 tons (around twelve times the tonnage of the *Titanic*) of British merchant vessels, while in the same month United Kingdom yards launched only 69,711 tons. More than ever the skills and capacity of the British shipbuilding industry were urgently needed. Lloyd George had replaced Asquith as Prime Minister in December 1916; he now overruled the admirals to introduce the convoy system which immediately did much to reduce losses. Harland and Wolff took a lead in the design and construction of 'standard' ships, simplified cargo vessels urgently needed to replace those lost at sea. The firm invested £1 million in 1917 primarily to build a new forty-one-acre yard on the east side of the Musgrave Channel, a ship-building yard equal in area to about forty football pitches. Harland and Wolff also built monitors for shelling coastal defences and two cruisers, one adapted as a seaplane carrier. In March 1918 Lloyd George appointed the firm's managing director, Lord Pirrie, as controller-general of merchant shipbuilding and under his direction output in the United Kingdom was raised by nearly fifty per cent by the time of the armistice.

During 1918 alone, Harland and Wolff launched 201,070 tons of merchant shipping, 120,000 tons more than the firm's nearest United Kingdom rival. Workman Clark built boom defence vessels, patrol boats, sloops and cargo ships totalling 260,000 tons during the war. Harland and Wolff broke all records in completing standard ships (merchant vessels built to a single design) – one was launched from Queen's Island on the morning of Tuesday 10th September 1918; by nightfall the engines and boilers were on board; and by 9 p.m. on Saturday it was ready for sea.

Feeding the Allied war machine

All the traditional export industries prospered, the Belfast Ropeworks, for example, producing fifty per cent of the Royal Navy's cordage requirements. James Mackie & Sons of Belfast, the largest manufacturer of linen machinery in the world, diversified to produce an estimated 75 million artillery shells.[44] There were new industries too.

PRONI - D3964/H/12A

Female munitions workers in James Mackie & Sons 1916.

IWM ART 2271

Shop for Machining 1918 by Anna Airy. A contemporary of William Orpen, Anna Airy was one of the first women artists employed by the newly founded Imperial War Museum in 1918. This was one of four large works, each representative of a typical scene at a munitions or armament factory.

In 1917 Lord Pirrie volunteered to open an aeroplane works, starting with six de Havilland machines, followed by one hundred Handley Page V/1500 heavy bombers for raiding Berlin, and three hundred Avros. He built an aerodrome on the site of a one hundred and seventy acre farm he bought at Aldergrove in Co Antrim. 'There is no pleasure like work,' the seventy-one-year-old entrepreneur said to a reporter in 1918.

[44] Keith Jeffery, 2000, p. 30

'I am never idle. I work all day.' Unlike most of his employees, Pirrie had been active supporter of Irish Home Rule. After the Easter Rebellion, however, he changed his mind in favour of partition.[45]

As the U-boat campaigns intensified, the importation of colonial produce became so hazardous that the population of the United Kingdom became ever more dependent on what food could be produced at home.

PRONI- AG/2/3/2/1

Farmers of County Derry!

INCREASE YOUR TILLAGE!

The County Committee of Agriculture, as your representatives, have pledged you to do so. They are quite confident that you will amply redeem that pledge.

GUARANTEE.—To protect you against the danger of loss the Government guarantee you the following prices for the 1917 crop :—1/7d per stone for Oats; and £5 15/- to £6 10/- per ton for Potatoes, according to date of delivery.

SEEDS.—If you have for sale, or require to purchase Seed Oats or Seed Potatoes, inform your Rural District Councillor, or the undersigned, AT ONCE.

MANURES.—Order IMMEDIATELY your Artificial Manures and Copper Sulphate from your merchant. These will not be any cheaper, and will most probably be unobtainable soon

IMPLEMENTS AND MACHINERY.—Order these NOW from the Local Agent. If you require a loan to purchase apply to the Committee.

COMPULSORY TILLAGE.—The Law requires occupiers of ten acres or over to till this season at least one-tenth of their arable land in addition to the area cultivated last year. Heavy penalties are attached for any default.

Inform the Committee of your wants, and they will advise you.

FARMERS OF DERRY! **It rests with you to make this County lead Ireland in the increased Production of Food in 1917.**

T. K. CALDWELL, Secretary,
County Londonderry Committee of Agriculture.

Courthouse, Coleraine. AG2/5/x/1

The numerous small farmers of Ireland (Ulster had a higher proportion of these than Munster or Leinster) successfully defied government attempts to regulate prices in a seller's market and enjoyed a prosperity they had never experienced before. Though eroded somewhat by wartime inflation, farm labourer wages rose by between sixty and seventy per cent during the war. Since the value of whitefish increased four-fold in value between 1914 and 1918, it is not surprising that the volume of the catch increased two thirds in weight.[46] Exhortations to plough grassland were largely unnecessary in Ulster. Farmers quickly realised that handsome profits could be made by growing flax once it became clear that the war was interrupting imported supplies. In the six north-eastern counties, arable land increased by more than 200,000 acres, much of it to grow flax.

Growing and processing flax was an exceptionally labour-intensive process. Planted in the spring and producing a delicate blue flower in early summer, flax was ready for harvesting around the middle of August. To ensure as long a fibre as possible, it was pulled, not cut, and then tied in sheaves, or

[45] Jonathan Bardon, 1992, pp 456–457

[46] Keith Jeffery, 2000, p. 31

beets, and allowed to dry in stooks for a few days. Then the beets were weighed down in a pond or dammed stream, known as a lint hole, and allowed to rot for about a fortnight, when they were raised (by men waist deep wielding forks almost overwhelmed by the disgusting smell) and spread on fields to dry. Only after the flax was 'broken', 'scutched' and 'hackled' – each process very laborious even with the assistance of machinery – could the fibres be made into thread: long fibres produced fine linen yarn, while short fibres were suitable for coarse cloth. Under employment had long been a problem in the Irish countryside: in Ulster it was all but banished now by the insatiable demand for flax to meet the needs of the linen industry.

PRONI - T3494

Thirty workers at Charters Spinning Mill Factory, North Howard St. Belfast 1915.

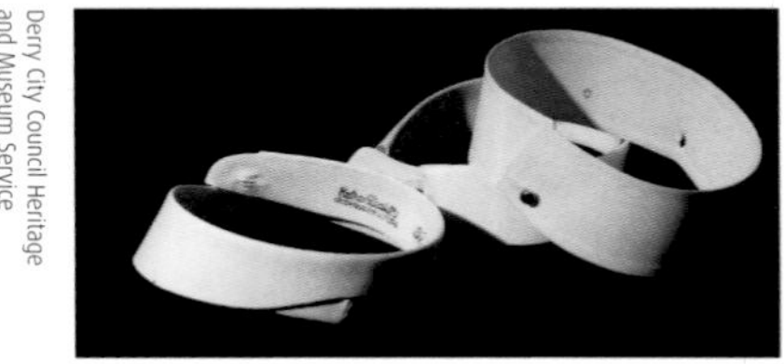

Derry City Council Heritage and Museum Service

Linen shirt collars

Across Ulster, and more particularly in Belfast and the Lagan valley, flax mills and linen factories worked at full stretch to fulfil government contracts for uniforms, tents, knapsacks, stretchers, awnings, sacking, fabric buckets, sheets and aeroplane fabric (the Ministry of Munitions placed contracts valued at over £11 million for this aircraft material alone). The workforce in this textile industry rose from 76,000 in 1913 to 90,000, around twenty per cent, by the end of the war. The Derry shirt-making trade also enjoyed a welcome revival, War Office contracts alone averaging nearly £830,000 each year of the war. In the first years of the war workers raised their living standards mainly by overtime payments, but by 1917 wages caught up with and then by-passed prices.

Women and the war

Unlike the rest of Ireland, the north-eastern corner of the island – just like Manchester and Leeds – had for long given employment in its mills and textile factories to women. Men made up only a small proportion of employees in the linen industry: about five out of every eight workers were female. Over ninety per cent of the workforce in the Derry shirt industry, the city's main employer, was female. During the war around 8,000 were employed: men supervised, cut the cloth, maintained the machines, and worked in the packing and dispatching departments; and women stitched the shirts together and did the processes associated with 'finishing'. Women's work in the United Kingdom's clothing industry was not acknowledged as skilled, but it was classed as skilled in the Derry shirt-making factories. It took four years to become a machinist clipping threads and experienced women had 'learners' observing what they were doing. There were then no fewer than twenty-five operations involved in stitching together and finishing a shirt, and some women became specialists concentrating on just a couple of these.[47]

PRONI - D3964/H/28

Sketch of woman *'Doing her bit'* c.1916, from a collection of photographs from the Albert Foundry Belfast.

The workforce in the province's engineering industry employed women for the first time during the war but the replacement of male labour by female labour was more muted in Ulster than it was on the other side of the Irish Sea. In England during the war the mass movement of women into munitions factories and engineering shops resulted in an acute shortage of females in domestic service. This does not seem to have happened in Ulster.

Women in the textile and shirt factories of Ulster saw their workforce increase by nearly twenty per cent between 1912 and 1916. Luxury

[47] Andrew Finlay, 'The Cutting Edge: Derry Shirtmakers', in C Curtin, P Jackson and B O'Connor (eds), *Gender in Irish Society*, Galway, 1987; Keith Jeffery, 2000, p.30

trades were depressed, however, resulting in women with specialist skills losing their employment. This caused so much concern that two central committees on women's employment were formed, one in Ulster under Lady Aberdeen, and the other for the other three provinces under the patronage of the Marchioness of Dufferin and Ava. These committees, and another set up by the Women's Emergency Suffrage Council, put women to work making such items as gloves and toys. Pay for this work was modest. However, at busy times of the year women were in demand as well-paid agricultural labourers, earning around £1 a week.[48] The price of eggs went up to two shillings a dozen by 1915 and since farmers' wives looked after the chickens and traditionally were allowed to keep money raised from the sale of eggs for themselves, the war brought them an unexpected bonus.

Derry City Council Heritage and Museum Service.

A Roll of Honour listing those who enlisted from Young and Rochester Ltd; a shirt, collar and cuff making factory in the Waterside area of Derry.

Women of all classes were involved in such activities as knitting socks and putting together packages for soldiers at the front. Girls went out over the bogs, especially in the vicinity of Omagh, to collect sphagnum moss to be dried and packed for surgical dressings. This natural material was valued for its absorbent and sterilising properties. Mary Pakenham recalled:

> *We had a special sort of two-ended sack which we hung round our necks like a stole and we went barefoot over the bog fishing the clumps of moss out of the pools. There were three sorts…After the stuff was got home it had to be dried and picked over…divided into graded compartments and lined with lily white paper.*

The formation of the Ulster Unionist Council in 1905 had been followed soon after by the setting up of the Ulster Women's Unionist Council. Once the war began, the UWUC was a ready-made support organisation for men who had volunteered to join the Ulster Division. On 11th August 1914 the UWUC offered the services of the UVF Nursing Corps and its dressing stations across Ulster. Thereafter the organisation volunteered to help take care of families and

[48] Caitriona Clear, 'Fewer ladies, more women', in John Horne (ed.), *Our War: Ireland and the Great War*, Dublin, 2008, pp 165–166

dependents of those who had joined up. The UWUC also had its own sphagnum moss depots and raised funds to buy motor ambulances to be presented to the Ulster Division.[49] The National Volunteers in Belfast also had a Nursing Corps. The Irish Women's Council of Belfast organised a recruiting event in St Mary's Hall in November 1914 and, before it began the Nursing Corps (NV) marched to the hall from the Falls Road to Divis Street in 'neat white uniforms with the red Cross and pretty rosettes of orange and green…with the splendid Craobh Ruadh pipers at their head'.[50]

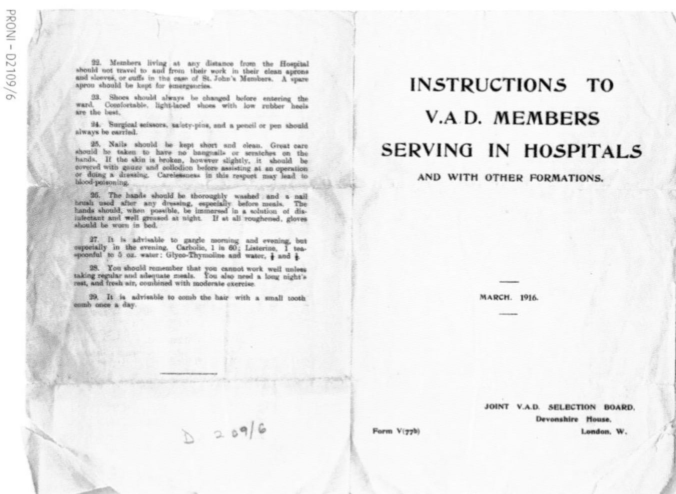

22. Members living at any distance from the Hospital should not travel to and from their work in their clean aprons and sleeves, or cuffs in the case of St. John's Members. A spare apron should be kept for emergencies.

23. Shoes should always be changed before entering the ward. Comfortable, light-laced shoes with low rubber heels are the best.

24. Surgical scissors, safety-pins, and a pencil or pen should always be carried.

25. Nails should be kept short and clean. Great care should be taken to have no hangnails or scratches on the hands. If the skin is broken, however slightly, it should be covered with gauze and collodion before assisting at an operation or doing a dressing. Carelessness in this respect may lead to blood-poisoning.

26. The hands should be thoroughly washed and a nail brush used after any dressing, especially before meals. The hands should, when possible, be immersed in a solution of disinfectant and well greased at night. If at all roughened, gloves should be worn in bed.

27. It is advisable to gargle morning and evening, but especially in the evening. Carbolic, 1 in 60; Listerine, 1 teaspoonful to 5 oz. water; Glyco-Thymoline and water, ½ and ½.

28. You should remember that you cannot work well unless taking regular and adequate meals. You also need a long night's rest, and fresh air, combined with moderate exercise.

29. It is advisable to comb the hair with a small tooth comb once a day.

D. 2109/6

INSTRUCTIONS TO V.A.D. MEMBERS SERVING IN HOSPITALS

AND WITH OTHER FORMATIONS.

MARCH. 1916.

Form V(77b)

JOINT V.A.D. SELECTION BOARD,
Devonshire House,
London, W.

Instruction manual for VAD members, March 1916.

Educated women for long had been frustrated at being confined to traditional supportive roles. Now the war opened up new opportunities. The carnage and mutilation of total war created an acute shortage of nurses. In addition to trained nurses, with several years' experience in hospital and district work,

[49] Eileen Reilly, 'Women and voluntary war work', in Adrian Gregory and Senia Pašeta (eds), *Ireland and the Great War: 'A War to Unite us All'?*, Manchester, 2002, pp 58–59 and p. 63

[50] Richard Grayson, 2009, p. 17

U.V.F. HOSPITAL.

UVF Hospital Belfast for wounded soldiers and sailors 1915.

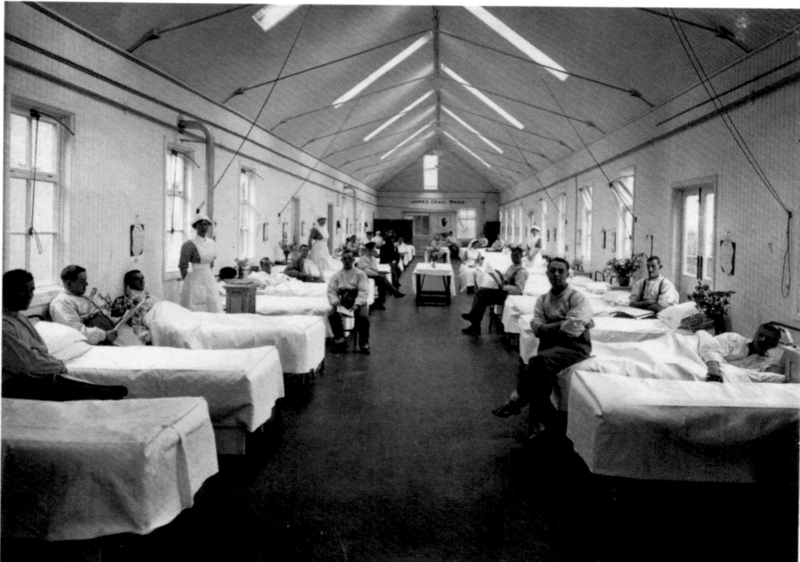

PRONI – INF/7/A/3/134

UVF Hospital Belfast for wounded soldiers and sailors 1915.

there were now temporary volunteers, known as Voluntary Aid Detachment (VAD) nurses. VAD nurses only got a three-month first-aid course with either the Red Cross or St John Ambulance. It is estimated that there were about 4,500 trained and voluntary Irish nurses serving in military medical organisations abroad. Rosabelle Osborne from Donegal had qualified at the turn of the century and became matron-in-chief at Salonika (now Thessaloniki) in 1917, in charge of twenty-six hospitals. A fifty-bed hospital at Pau in southern France, under the patronage of the Duchess of Abercorn, became so popular with VADs that it had to turn away many of those nurses who applied, even though one of the qualifications insisted on was the ability to speak French.[51]

Royal Ulster Rifles Museum

Teddy Bear made by an Irish soldier recovering from wounds, for Mrs SF McConnell, the nurse who cared for him.

[51] Catriona Clear, 2008, pp 161–163

Chapter 8 FROM MESSINES TO THE ARMISTICE, AND AFTER

Side by side at Wytschaete

The year 1917 saw some striking changes. The United States joined the Allies in the war. After a brilliant but costly summer offensive against Austria-Hungary in 1916, Russia was paralysed by revolution in the autumn of 1917. The Royal Navy tightened its blockade of commerce reaching Germany which resulted in near famine conditions there and in Austria during the 'turnip winter' of 1917–18. In 1917 the butcher's bill for both sides on the Western Front was appalling, without victory for either side.

Memorial of three Irish Divisions, 36th (Ulster) Division, 16th (Irish) Division and 10th (Irish) Division at the Island of Ireland Peace Park in Messines, Belgium.

One significant Allied success, Messines, involved Irishmen north and south. The battle began with the detonation of high explosives laboriously put in place by coal miners excavating long shafts. Nineteen mines were detonated with devastating success. Claud Potter was there:

> *I shall never forget seeing the St Eloi, Hill 60 and Messines mines going up… The ground swayed under us like an earthquake, followed by huge sheets of red and yellow flame and columns of debris and black smoke. The barrage was a fine sight too… Very little Hun retaliation…*
>
> *We can't make out what was wrong with Fritz. He put up no fight at all. What happened to his guns?… Hun lines fearfully knocked about and wire flattened…*[52]

Then the 36th (Ulster) Division and the 16th (Irish) Division took joint action, sweeping forward to overcome German lines and to capture the German strong-point of Wytschaete. 'The Rout of the Hun was very complete', Major H F N Jourdain, 6th Connaughts, noted in his diary on 8th June. Private Jack Christie, a Shankill UVF man who had joined the Ulster Division, observed afterwards:

> *We should never let politics blind us to the truth about things – bravery and loyalty wasn't all on one side. The 16th Division played a vital part alongside us.*

The close cooperation of the two divisions at Messines was poignantly illustrated by a high-profile casualty. Aged 56 in 1917, Willy Redmond, brother of the Irish Party leader and himself a Nationalist MP, was reputedly the oldest captain in the British Army, serving in the 6th Royal Irish Regiment in the 16th Division. On 7th June, against advice, he led his men into combat only to be severely wounded. He was brought in by Private John Meeke, an Ulster Division stretcher-bearer, to an aid post where Redmond died after being given the last rites by a Catholic chaplain in that division.[53]

---

[52] John Potter, 2013, p. 96

[53] Richard Grayson, 2009, p. 109, p. 115, and pp 116–118

Character certificate, discharge papers and medals belonging to Sergeant Christopher John Carr.

John Redmond received dozens of letters of condolence, one of them from Major Henry Allen, Unionist MP for North Armagh:

> *...it was only a few weeks ago that he and I travelled over to England...on that occasion he was in one of his most characteristically cheerful moods and kept myself and half a dozen MPs of all persuasions in roars of laughter with his sallies and jokes. It isn't every man of fifty-six who is willing to 'take on' such a war as this present one – your brother not only did so, but gallantly made fun of every aspect of it...*

Though he was awarded a Military Medal for his bravery at Messines, Private Meeke was buried in an unmarked grave in Derrykeighan Cemetery in north Antrim when he died in 1923. In 2004 the Bushmills historian, Robert Thompson, raised funds to have a proper headstone erected. John Meeke was buried beside his brother Samuel, who had returned to Ulster a dying man, his health broken after been forced to work in sulphur mines as a German prisoner of war.[54]

The Battle of Messines was a hopeful prelude to the terrible and protracted trench warfare at Passchendaele, the 3rd battle of Ypres. In 1918, when the Bolsheviks took Russia out of the war, the Germans concentrated to make one last attempt to break through the Western Front. On the morning of 21st March, storm trooper battalions broke through Allied lines east of the Somme. Holding positions east of Peronne, the 16th (Irish) Division was almost totally destroyed in this offensive. The division's nine under-strength battalions suffered an average of ten per cent fatalities. By the night of 3rd April, when it was relieved, it had the highest casualties of any division fighting in this theatre since 21st March – 7,149 killed, wounded and missing.[55] During this 'Spring Offensive' the Germans pushed the Allied lines back forty miles and their great howitzer, 'Big Bertha', got close enough to shell Paris. Troops of the 6th Connaughts

---

[54] *Ballymoney and Moyle Times*, 28th October 2004; Dermot Meleady, *John Redmond: The National Hero*, Sallins, 2014, pp 140–141. With thanks to Alister McReynolds for supplying this information

[55] Dermot Meleady, 2014, p. 457

and the 2nd Leinsters, along with the Belfast men of the 2nd Royal Irish Rifles, were amongst those attempting to hold a fluid and fragile defensive line. In the end, however, the Germans were exhausted and had over-extended their supply lines. The Allies made well-coordinated flanking counterattacks, aided by hundreds of tanks, and pushed the Germans back and back.

This turning of the tide was accomplished to a considerable extent by a much better and broader appreciation by the Allies than by the Germans of the 'all-arms' battle, in which artillery played an even greater role than tanks: this involved the skilful coordination of ground forces – armour, field guns and infantry – with careful use of information provided by aerial observation. Elsewhere, meanwhile, the Turkish and Austro-Hungarian empires were falling apart, Italy at last won a great victory at Vittorio Veneto and the U-boat campaign had been defeated.

Enniskillen and the Armistice

The Germans signed an armistice in a railway carriage in Compiègne and the guns fell silent at 11 a.m. on 11th November 1918. Oddly enough, Enniskillen was perhaps the first place in the United Kingdom to hear of the armistice. Having picked up a faint radio message at 6.30 a.m., troops in the barracks there spread the news by launching rockets and soon church bells rang out to greet crowds gathering for the hiring fair.[56]

Perhaps as many as ten million had lost their lives in this world war.[57] Recently some historians have concluded that the figure of those who met with violent deaths in this conflict should be much higher. At least 170,000 Irishmen enlisted during the war – some forty-one per cent of the male population between the ages of 10 and 44 in the 1911 census – and about half of them were from Ulster.

---

[56] Brian Barton, *Brookeborough: The Making of a Prime Minister*, Belfast, 1988, p. 26

[57] *Economist*, 29th March 2014, pp 87–91; 'Oh, What a Lovely Myth', Max Hastings, *Sunday Times* News Review, 11th May 2014

Nearly 28,000 Irishmen– and, indeed, boys – who had joined up in Ireland never returned. It is impossible to give an accurate figure of how many of the 28,000 were from Ulster. In addition, a great many Irishmen from both north and south joined British regiments and were to fight and die with them, thus increasing the island's overall death-toll. Other Irishmen fought and died in forces sent by the dominions of the British Empire, raising the final figure of the fallen still more. The historian, William Sheehan, reckons that the war cost the lives of 35,000 Irishmen. Neil Richardson concludes that 'thirty-five to fifty thousand Irishmen lost their lives'. The most recent figure, agreed by Irish academic historians writing in May 2014, is 49,646 Irishmen killed in the First World War. Of these Irish fallen, no place of birth was recorded for 7,405. Another 11,255 Irishmen killed in this conflict, and included in the 49,646 figure, were of Irish parentage but born in Britain and in other parts of the world. The breakdown – which does not include 741 men simply recorded as being from Ireland – for each Ulster county is as follows:

Antrim	**5,221**
Armagh	**1,117**
Cavan	**421**
Donegal	**700**
Down	**2,048**
Londonderry	**1,357**
Fermanagh	**498**
Monaghan	**343**

[58]

The Spanish influenza epidemic which swept the world as the war came to a close may have taken more lives than all those slain on all the battlefields put together in over four years of conflict. A particular feature of this pandemic was that those with the strongest immune

[58] 'Ireland at War', Centenary Magazine, Part 1, *Irish Independent*, 10th May 2014

systems were especially vulnerable – the young and fit were the ones most likely to die of the virus.[59]

Some of those who took part in this war are difficult to categorise. The author's great uncle, George Bardon, had emigrated to Australia. On the outbreak of war he attempted to join up but the Australian Army turned him down because he had a slight 'weakness of heart, after typhoid'. The following year he was accepted into the 11th Australian Infantry Battalion and sailed for Europe. He missed the Gallipoli campaign but joined the ANZAC forces on the Western Front. Though often in the thick of many engagements, he survived the fighting. Then in 1918 he was given leave to visit his family in Dublin. There he caught Spanish influenza and died in Dublin, buried with full military honours in the Grangegorman Military Cemetery alongside other Irishmen in the Australian forces who, unlike him, had fallen in combat on the Allied side.[60]

The future was uncertain for survivors returned to Ireland. A great many had lost limbs and otherwise been terribly wounded; others suffered from what was then described as 'shell shock'; men who expected to have first choice in jobs when they returned were faced with mass unemployment after the post-war boom had collapsed in the winter of 1920-1921 (in the 1920s a fifth, and in the 1930s a quarter, of male workers, insured under the 1911 and 1920 National Insurance Acts, were unemployed in Northern Ireland); and so many ex-servicemen did not get the recognition for putting their lives in danger that they expected.

Royal Ulster Rifles Museum

The Memorial Plaque was issued after the First World War to the next-of-kin of all British and Empire service personnel who were killed as a result of the war.

The plaques, made of bronze, became known as the *Dead Man's Penny*, because of the similarity in appearance to the somewhat smaller penny coin.

[59] Neil Richardson, *A Coward if I Return, a Hero if I Fall: Stories of Irishmen in World War 1*, Dublin, 2010, p. 300; Sheehan, 2011, dustcover; Neil Richardson, 2010, p. 234; Jonathan Bardon, 2008, p. 441; for the influenza epidemic in Belfast, Jonathan Bardon, 1992, pp 460–461

[60] 'An Irishman's Diary', Kieran Fagan, *Irish Times*, 11th November 2003

'I was to become a soldier of a very different sort'

The civil war which threatened Ireland in 1914 began in January 1919. Now men returned from the front, many inured to violence by the horrors of trench warfare, to renew their fighting in Ireland. Robert Lynd, an Ulsterman who was then a correspondent of the English *Daily News*, reported that 'soldiers who fought for the Allies as they return home are becoming converted by the thousand into Sinn Feiners', some, like the Gallipoli veteran, Tom Barry, to become leading men in the IRA. Returning soldiers played a crucial role in reviving the Ulster Volunteer Force, particularly in Derry city. 'I had thought my soldiering days were over', wrote Captain Sir Basil Brooke, the Fermanagh landlord awarded the Military Cross during the war; '...I was to become a soldier of a very different sort...but I had the added stimulant of defending my own birthplace'.

PEACE CELEBRATIONS

CHILDREN'S SPORTS.

Admit one child to the Sports to be held at the Castle Grounds on SATURDAY, the 19th JULY, at 12 o'clock.

Children will assemble on the Esplanade at 11-30 a.m., and, headed by a Band, will march up Main Street, along Hamilton Road, to the Ward Park.

At the Park gates they will receive a peace celebration medal, and will then march through the Park to the Castle Street entrance of the Castle Grounds, where those wearing medals will be handed a bag of Cakes and a bottle of Lemonade.

Only children wearing a Medal will be admitted to the Grounds, and only those with a ticket will receive a medal. KEEP THIS TICKET.

SPECTATOR

PRONI-LA/20/50

Armistice event in Bangor

The Anglo-Irish War edged into Ulster in the spring of 1920 as blood was shed in internecine warfare in Derry. During that summer Belfast, Lisburn, Banbridge and Dromore were convulsed by intercommunal conflict and intimidation. Northern Ireland was created in December 1920 by the Government of Ireland Act. Then, following protracted negotiations after the IRA had agreed to a truce in July 1921, the Anglo-Irish Treaty was signed in 10 Downing Street on 6th December 1921: this agreement created the Irish Free State as a self-governing dominion of the British Empire. The blood-letting did not cease until the spring of 1923. In the six counties of what became Northern Ireland the death toll between July 1920 and July 1922 was 577 – 303 Catholics, 172 Protestants and 82 members of the security forces.

In Belfast alone, 236 people had been killed in the first months of 1922, more than in the widespread troubles in Germany in the same period.[61]

[61] Jonathan Bardon, 1992, pp 466–467, and p. 495; Brian Barton, 1988, p. 28

Those who had been cheered off to war in 1914 by Home Rule supporters and survived to return to their native land, did not receive the thanks they felt they had a right to expect. The future in the south lay with separatists. In the 1918 general election Joseph Devlin retained his West Belfast seat but he was one of just six Nationalists returned to Westminster (Sinn Féin won 73 seats and Unionists 26). Those who had answered his call to join up in 1914 returned to their communities only to find that it was best to remain silent on their war service.

The protracted amnesia about the participation of so many in the Great War was ended in 2002 when, before television cameras, two Belfast men, the loyalist David Ervine and the republican Tom Hartley, together toured the war cemeteries along the Western Front; and in May 2011 when, side by side, Queen Elizabeth II and Mary McAleese, President of Ireland, laid wreaths and paid tribute to Irishmen, north and south, who had given their lives in that most terrible conflict.

Suggested Further Reading

Bardon, Jonathan, *A History of Ulster*, Belfast, 1992

Barton, Brian, *Brookeborough: The Making of a Prime Minister*, Belfast, 1988

Bowman, Timothy, *The Irish regiments in the Great War – Discipline and Morale*, Manchester, 2006

Buckland, Geoffrey, *James Craig, Lord Craigavon*, Dublin, 1980

Coffey, David (ed.), *David Thompson writes home: Letter of a Newtown Lad*, 1914–16, Newtownards

Dawe, Gerald, *An Anthology of Irish War Poetry 1914–1945*, Belfast, 2008

Denman, Terence, *Ireland's Unknown Soldiers: The 16th (Irish) Division in the Great War*, Dublin 1992

Falls, Cyril, *The history of the 36th (Ulster) Division*, 1922, London

Fanning, Ronan, *Fatal Path: British Government and Irish Revolution 1910–1922*, London, 2013

Grayson, Richard, *Belfast Boys: How Unionists and Nationalists fought and died together in the First World War*, London, 2009

Gregory, Adrian and Senia Paseta (eds), *Ireland and the Great War: 'A War to Unite us All'?*, Manchester, 2002

Hastings, Max, *Catastrophe: Europe Goes to War 1914*, London, 2013

Horne, John (ed.), *Our War: Ireland and the Great War*, Dublin, 2008

'Ireland at War', Centenary Magazines, *Irish Independent*, Part 1 10 May 2014, Part 2, 17 May 2014

Jeffery, Keith, *Ireland and the Great War*, Cambridge, 2000
Field Marshal Sir Henry Wilson: a political soldier, Oxford, 2006

Laffan, Michael, *The Partition of Ireland 1911–1925*, Dundalk, 1983

Meleady, Dermot, *John Redmond: The National Leader*, Sallins, 2014

Orr, Philip, *The Road to the Somme: Men of the Ulster Division Tell their Story*, Belfast, 1987
Field of Bones: an Irish Division at Gallipoli, Dublin, 2006

Parkhill, Trevor, *The First World War Diaries of Emma Duffin, Belfast Voluntary Aid Detachment Nurse*, Dublin, 2014

Potter, John, *Scarce Heard Amid The Guns: the experiences of a Gunner officer in the First World War as recorded in his diary and letters home*, Belfast, 2013

Richardson, Neil, *A Coward if I Return, a Hero if I Fall: Stories of Irishmen in World War 1*, Dublin, 2010

Sheehan, William, *The Western Front: Irish Voices from the Great War*, Dublin, 2011

Stewart, A T Q, *The Ulster Crisis*, London, 1967
Edward Carson, Dublin, 1981

White, Stuart N, *The Terrors: 16th (Pioneer) Battalion Royal Irish Rifles*, (Somme Association), Belfast, 1996

Jonathan Bardon

Dr Jonathan Bardon was born in Dublin in 1941 and was brought up and educated in that city. After graduating in Modern History and Political Science at Trinity College Dublin in 1963, he moved to Belfast where he has spent almost all of his adult life. He began his teaching career in Orangefield Boys Secondary School before becoming a further education lecturer in and senior manager in what became the Belfast College of Business Studies and is now Belfast Metropolitan College. Between 1999 and 2007 he was employed in the School of History in Queen's University Belfast.

His books include: *A History of Ulster* (1992); *From GI Brides to the Modern Family – 65 Years of Relate NI* (2014); *The Plantation of Ulster* (2011); *A History of Ireland in 250 Episodes* (2008); *Belfast A Century* (1999); *Investigating Place Names in Ulster* (1991); *Belfast: an illustrated History* (1982); *Dublin: A Thousand Years of Wood Quay* (1984); *The Belfast Charitable Society 1752–2002* (2003); *The Struggle for Shared Schools in Northern Ireland* (2009); *Beyond the Studio: A History of BBC Northern Ireland* (2000); and *The Struggle for Ireland: 400–1450 AD* (1970).

He has written historical documentaries for Channel 4 and the BBC, including: *Understanding Northern Ireland*, ten twenty-minute television documentaries for Channel 4; one hour television documentaries on the Belfast Blitz and the 1798 rebellion for BBC Northern Ireland; and 48 twenty-minute and 360 five-minute programmes on the history of Ireland for BBC Radio Ulster.

He has lectured on Irish history in the USA, Canada, Romania, Germany and Belgium, in addition to many venues in Great Britain and Ireland. He was chairman of the NI Community Relations Council (1996– 2002) and was awarded an OBE in 2003.

NORTHERN IRELAND
WAR MEMORIAL

LED BY IWM